HOW TO BE A PERSON IN THE WORLD

Also by Heather Havrilesky

Disaster Preparedness

HOW TO BE A PERSON IN THE WORLD

—m—

Ask Polly's Guide Through the Paradoxes of Modern Life

Heather Havrilesky

Doubleday

New York · *London* · *Toronto*
Sydney · *Auckland*

www.doubleday.com

DOUBLEDAY and the portrayal of an anchor with a dolphin are
registered trademarks of Penguin Random House LLC.

Several pieces first appeared, in slightly different form, in the following
publications: *The Awl*, Ask Polly (www.theawl.com): "The Cheat Sheet" originally
published as "Give Me One Reason Why I Shouldn't Cheat On My Wife?"
(July 10, 2013), "Mourning Glory" originally published as "Last Year My Dad
Died Unexpectedly and I Can't Get Over It" (April 30, 2014), "That Bitter
Aftertaste" originally published as "I Feel Bitter About All My Exes and I Can't
Get Over It" (August 28, 2013), "What Would Kanye Do?" originally published
as "How Do I Find True Love and Stop Dating Half-Assed Men?" (October 16,
2013), and "Why Don't the Men I Date Ever Love Me?" originally published
as "Why Don't the Men I Date Ever Truly Love Me?" (September 3, 2014).
New York magazine's blog, The Cut (http://nymag.com/thecut/): "The Bean
Eaters" originally published as "Aging Is Scary and Life Is a Struggle. Why
Keep Going?" (September 17, 2014), "Career or Baby?" originally published
as "Should I Have a Baby or Establish My Career First?" (April 15, 2015), and
"Making Friends (Out of Nothing at All)" originally published as "How Am I
Supposed to Make Friends in My Late 20's?" (August 27, 2014).

Jacket design by Emily Mahon

Library of Congress Cataloging-in-Publication Data

Havrilesky, Heather.
How to be a person in the world : ask Polly's guide through the paradoxes of
modern life / Heather Havrilesky.—1 Edition.
pages   cm
ISBN 978-0-385-54039-1 (hardcover)—ISBN 978-0-385-54040-7 (eBook)
1. Self-actualization (Psychology) I. Title.
BF637.S4.H3757 2016
070.4'44—dc23
2015023592

MANUFACTURED IN THE UNITED STATES OF AMERICA
First Edition

For Bill, Ivy, Claire, and Zeke

Contents

Author's Note

In the fall of 2012, I pitched an existential advice column to *The Awl*, a website that publishes smart, original takes on modern culture. At the time, I was a regular contributor to the *New York Times Magazine*, writing mostly essays about pop culture, and I had a column called the Best-Seller List in *Bookforum*. I'd spent seven years as a TV critic for Salon.com, I'd written a cartoon called *Filler* for Suck.com (the Internet's first daily website!) for five years before that, and I'd answered advice letters on my own blog as early as 2001.

But this was something new. I'd never dished up advice to a wider audience. When *The Awl*'s co-founder, Choire Sicha, said yes to my idea, he made it clear that the column could be anything I wanted it to be. But what did I want it to be? Obviously, I had all kinds of outspoken, sometimes unwelcome advice to offer friends, family, and complete strangers alike. I'd been handing out unsolicited advice for years. But did I want the column to be funny? Did I want to use the column to rail against the scourge of passivity and avoidance in modern relationships or to address our culture's burdensome fixation on constant self-improvement? Did I want to sneak in some commentary on troubled friendships, Kanye West, weddings, rescue dogs, luxe brands, commitmentphobic men, property ownership, the artist's life, pushy mothers-in-law, or *Game of Thrones*?

As it turned out, I wanted to do all of these things, and eventually I did. But when I was sitting down to write my first weekly column, I just felt scared. "Who do I think I am, giving other people advice?" I thought. "I'm not qualified for this! I don't have it all figured out. What the hell am I doing?"

I've been asking myself that same question every week for four years now. And when Stella Bugbee, the editorial director for *New York* magazine's website *The Cut,* approached me about taking my advice column over to her site, I wondered what she was thinking. Sure, this meant a much larger audience for Ask Polly and more money for me. But did she really know what she was signing on to? "You know my column is three thousand words long every week, and half of those words are 'fuck,' right?" I asked her. Somehow, this didn't scare her off.

I don't always feel qualified to guide other people to a better life. As a writer, even when I'm sitting down to start a book review or a cultural essay, as I've done professionally for years now, the blank page mocks me. "What could *you* possibly have to say?" it asks. "When are you going to give this up and do something useful with your life?" The blank page can be a real asshole sometimes.

Still, nothing I do brings me more happiness than writing Ask Polly. I'm not always sure of the right answer for any letter, whether someone is dealing with depression and anxiety, a go-nowhere job, a series of not-quite boyfriends, or an overly critical parent. But I do know for certain that when I reach out as far as I can to another person, using my words—my awkward, angry, uplifting, uncertain, joyful, clumsy words (half of which are still "fuck")—some kind of magic happens. There is magic that comes from reaching out. I don't believe in many things, but I believe in that, with all of my heart.

HOW TO BE A PERSON IN THE WORLD

I

Flaws Become You

Here Comes the (Anxious) Bride

Dear Polly,

I am getting married in June, and I am the first child in my family to be getting married. I have a younger brother and a younger sister, both of whom I am very close with. Throughout the wedding planning process, I have tried to be very nondramatic and very non-Bridezilla-y, but when my sister (also my maid of honor) recently asked if she could bring her foreign boyfriend to meet my parents for the first time and also attend the wedding, I immediately and adamantly refused her.

My sister, since entering college, has far and away been considered the hot sister. When we are together, other people, including our own relatives and family friends, often mistake her for the older sister because she looks more mature and sophisticated. Not only is she a talented amateur photographer, but she also spent a gap year in Europe and is now trilingual. She also managed to get into the Ivy League that my parents wish I had gotten into, and enjoys the kind of popularity I have never experienced in my life (nor will I ever experience). I, on the other hand, could aptly be considered the nerdy sister, who was smart and always did things the "right" way but will never be glamorous or nearly as interesting. We were never that competitive as children, because our age gap made a big difference then, but now I have absurd conniptions of jealousy whenever my sister posts gorgeous pictures from her parties and travels.

When my sister was in Europe last year, she acquired a very attractive, older foreign boyfriend. No one in my family was convinced it would last, but now they are still together and seem pretty serious. My sister skipped Christmas to spend it abroad with him. Now she suddenly wants him to meet all of us in the States. And she wants it to happen my wedding weekend.

When I think about this happening, my head implodes, because I know all our relatives and mutual friends will be stunned by how gorgeous she and her perfect boyfriend look together. Because she has never introduced him to anyone, this will mean extra excitement that will almost certainly steal the spotlight from my wedding—my party, which I want to be about ME. I know this all sounds petty and selfish, but if there's ever a time in your life you get to be a little bit selfish, it's at your own goddamn wedding. And I just can't shake the idea that if I let her bring him, their stupid-perfect luminosity will overshadow everything else. I also know that my refusal is almost entirely due to my own insecurities . . . but you only get married once. Her boyfriend can meet everyone at another time, right? Am I being insanely mean for not letting him come to the wedding? Is it okay for me to be selfish this time, or will I regret this later?

Selfish Bride

—⟋⟍—

Dear Selfish Bride,

Yes, you can be selfish at your own goddamn wedding. You can invite anyone you want and wear anything you want and serve exactly what you love to eat. Hell, if you wanted to, you could release twenty-one white doves and then shoot them all out of the sky with a shotgun, one by one. Fuck it! It's your day to be the most beautiful fairy princess in the whole universe! It's your day to shine!

And let's just admit it, no matter how much we try to rise

above it, most of us do have this strange little desire to be the most glamorous creature on the face of the planet for just one day. ONE GODDAMN DAY, THAT'S ALL WE ASK! Can you really blame us? Did we not grow up in this idiotic airbrushed-lip-glossy-goddess-adoring culture? How many Disney movies and beauty pageants and episodes of *The Bachelor* can you watch before some sick corner of your brain calcifies into an absurd desire to be a gorgeous, shiny sparkle princess *for just one day?*

Here's the awful truth, though. Some of us just aren't any good at pulling off the sparkle-princess thing. We can't manage it. Sure, if we were surrounded by a team of expensive stylists and trainers and nutritionists and managers and fluffers at all times, we might be able to do it. If we had highly paid service professionals who handed us tall glasses of iced lemon water and fluffed our hair and rubbed pig fetuses into our crow's-feet every few milliseconds, then we *might* pull off something faintly approximating glamour and poise and glittery perfection.

But on your wedding day, instead of being surrounded by fawning helper types, you're going to find yourself surrounded by your family. Your FAMILY, for fuck's sake. Not to mention your self-involved, bitch-ass friends. And even though your friends are so supportive and loving that they'll volunteer to help make sure you don't get a terrible updo from the hairstylist (who will look just like Dolly Parton, by the way), instead they're going to take off to have lunch and leave you alone and your hair is going to get uglier and uglier, with all these curly tendrils forming like you're an early '80s Olympic figure skater. But you're going to be so hungry and nervous and unhinged that you won't say a word, you'll just start weeping and snotting into your hands and your $150 makeup job will smear, but you won't be able to stop crying and you'll text your friends "HELP!" and they'll say, "BACK IN A SEC," but they won't be back until thirty minutes later, and by then you'll look like Hermione Granger at the Yule Ball meets Divine post-monsoon. And then you'll go to your room and pace and freak out and wonder why you decided to participate in a stressful $18,000 three-ring circus when you two could've just gone to City Hall and had a burger afterwards. And when you finally walk down the aisle and say your vows, your husband-to-be won't have set up the mic, so no one will be able to hear a word and it'll be 110 degrees outside and you'll be wearing a gown that basically feels like a comforter strapped to your body, so your ass will be soaked in sweat and you'll need to use the bathroom, and everyone you know will be there, staring at you, feeling sorry for you because you're so awkward and so greasy and so old, and JESUS IT'S A MIRACLE SHE FOUND ANY-ONE, HOW'D SHE TRICK THIS GUY INTO MARRYING HER ANYWAY?

So please, allow me to ruin your special day for you right here, right now, because it will get ruined no matter what with your current attitude. That's the irony of the selfish bride who just wants to be a shiny happy glowing Bride Barbie for one day. The harder you try to make that dream happen, the more of a nightmare your special day will become. Mark my words. You cannot be calm and relaxed *and* be the prettiest and most important and most enviable woman in the world, not even for just one day. You can't! Your dream will not come true. Maybe if you had a million dollars to spend and you had a bunch of jackbooted thugs who forced your sister to wear no makeup and dress in rags and leave the hot, exotic boyfriend at home, you could pull it off. And maybe if your thugs could also force all of the guests to gasp and sigh when you entered, and they could bust in the kneecaps of anyone who dared to make a sound at the sight of your sister. Maybe if you handed out a script to every one of your friends. Maybe if the lighting were just so, and you gave everyone a pre-ceremony Valium. Maybe if you had an animation studio do a CGI version of your wedding so everything came out just right. Maybe if you could just uninvite your entire family.

Barring all that, you will not get your one glorious day to shine. And the more you try to control all of the variables, the less happy you'll be on your wedding day. The more you think, "This is my day! It must go perfectly!" the less you'll be able to experience the real point of the day, which is to celebrate not just you, in all of your beautiful but merely mortal wonder, but also to celebrate your brand-new husband, and your mother and father and your husband's family and your siblings and his siblings and your cousins and his cousins, and YES, EVEN YOUR SISTER'S BRAND-NEW HANDSOME GUY. Weddings are all about anyone who cares enough to buy a stupid preselected gift and drag their ass to the event. The end.

So stop it. Call your sister, and tell her you were temporarily rendered unwell by an asshole virus and you actually want her boyfriend to come to the wedding after all. You're looking forward to meeting him, in fact. With this act, you will instantly, like MAGIC, render yourself fifteen times more beautiful and glowing on your wedding day. Yes, you can say to your sister, "Look, I'm insecure and worried about this day. Can you help me to stay calm and look nice? And can you try not to look just like a supermodel that day and try to look like a regular person instead? I know that's weak and lame of me, but can you help me?" Have a good fucking cry while you're at it. For some reason, I'm guessing that your sister, if she really is the sensitive bohemian you portray her to be, will find your vulnerability touching and she'll step up her whole game to make your day more special.

I have an older sister, and though I was far from the goddess you describe your sister as, I think she sometimes considered herself the nerdier one of the two of us when we were younger. (And please note, while I'm here dispensing advice, she is a cancer surgeon who saves lives.) I still remember the day of her wedding, when she was anxious about putting on more than the faintest glimmer of blush. "No, that looks fake," she'd say and wipe it off. It was really cute. Today, I have two photos of my sister's wedding in my house, and just one photo of my own wedding. In the photo from my wedding, I'm sitting on a rock in my white comforter, talking to two little kids, my brand-new nieces, and I'm wincing as if to say, "Do I have to pretend to care about children now?" I still remember how my legs were sweating profusely and I wanted to maybe throw up or lay down for a while.

But in my sister's wedding photos, my sister looks so natural and happy and just . . . I know it's a cliché, but she looks angelic. She is luminous. She really is. No one went out of their way to tell me I looked nice that day or paid special attention to the new boyfriend I had with me. Everyone was too busy being enchanted by my sister. They were all just thrilled to see her so happy.

I get a good feeling whenever I look at her photos. She was so generous and patient with me that weekend—even though I was feeling a little sorry for myself because my new boyfriend was flirting with all of the bridesmaids. My sister never acted like the whole day was about her. If anything, she seemed to want to share her big day with me.

I'm not trying to criticize you. I just want you to take a minute to picture what it would be like for your sister's stupid-perfect luminosity to spoil everything, just like you suspect it will, and I want you to get over it. I want you to think about what it would be like if you ever lost her, how much that would crush you like a bug into the ground, and how much you'd regret your behavior right now. I want you to expect that she *will* upstage you, accept it, and find a way to enjoy your imperfect day anyway. Because you won't have another shot at sharing your big day with grace and generosity and kindness.

And ultimately, so what? It's just a fucking wedding. It's your day to ruin, if you feel like ruining it. But I wouldn't recommend that. I would work hard to change your attitude. I would reverse your decision and apologize to your sister.

Stop thinking of it as YOUR day. You're the hostess, after all! What a terrible day to be gorgeous and reign supreme when you can't even soak it in because you have to run around and kiss uncles and chat up cousins the whole time. If you really want to be a gorgeous princess shining from on high, figure out another day to do it. At your wedding, just be as generous and gracious and kind as you can possibly be. Nothing could be more beautiful than that.

Polly

My Mind Likes Imagining Boys

Polly,

I want to be single right now. Completely, deliciously, misandrist-ically single—not giving a solitary thought to men, much less actively dating them. So why can't I get them out of my head?

I visited a friend last month to get away from the city and get clear on my feelings about my stumbling relationship. My friend introduced me to her cute friend, who I thought might be a little into her, but I may have misread it since they live in a small community, so sometimes friendships can get pretty intimate. She showed no sign of being interested in him, so I felt no weirdness saying, as we were wrapping up our visit, "I feel like my relationship with my boyfriend is winding down, and if we break up, I definitely don't want to date for a while. But I have to say, just out of admiration, that your friend is mad cute." To which she responded, "I'm so glad you said that because I spent all weekend thinking what a good couple the two of you would make! Of course you would want to be single for as long as you need, but when you're ready to date again, I could definitely hook you two up."

Three weeks later, I do break up with my boyfriend, ready to be completely without men. Yet, in the absence of a relationship, my brain keeps drifting to this friend of a friend, making up scenarios about him whenever it feels bored or lonely. I try to clear my mind of all things manly, and yet there he is. I'd already scheduled a postmortem call with my friend to go over the breakup, and I decide that during our chat I'll ask her to give me the friend of a friend's e-mail address so when I'm ready, I can see if he's interested. If I can't stop making up brain stories about him, I might as well look forward to asking him out someday in the future.

So my friend and I hop on the call, and the first thing she says is, "I have to tell you something—friend of a friend and I are dating!"

Oh. Congratulations. How wonderful.

I'm upset. I'm upset? I'm upset! And I feel like an idiot for feeling that way! I've only been around this guy for a weekend, and apparently my brain can't just sit around being brilliant; it has to weave a rich fucking tapestry of what-ifs and expectations until I actually have skin in a game that I barely know anything about!

I know I'll feel better about this in a few days, Polly. But my brain has always been like this—rich fucking tapestries are sort of its specialty—and I don't want to keep repeating the process of hopes created by my brain being dashed by other people's completely reasonable behaviors. Help me make my mind a superspecial top secret no-boys-allowed club.

Love,
De-Men Be Gone

—⊶⊷—

Dear DMBG,

Hot damn, do I feel you! What a waste, to focus all of the brilliant colors of your overactive imagination on some random dude-canvas over and over again. That's like weaving a rich tapestry and then using it as a dog bed. (Not that I wouldn't do that in a heartbeat. If I could weave.)

I was a mind weaver of rich fucking tapestries, too, back in the day, with some demure yet straight-talkin', slightly slimmer, slightly more hygienic version of my actual self right there at the center of it all and the imaginary dude of the month right next to me, looking both hotter and saner than he ever did in real life. In these ancient daydream textiles, I was always saying sexy things and flashing my sparkly eyes, and the dude was always guffawing at my ribald humor or gasping at my beauty like he was hooked to an IV of bourbon, Percocet, fine Colombian coffee, and fine Colombian cocaine. All I needed to create these vibrant dreamscapes was a glancing encounter with a random attractive friend-of-a-friend type of dude, and it was ON. And hours and hours of private storytelling and imaginings and pointless mind exercises later—in which said random dude repeatedly treasured every syllable out of my glossy lips, then ravished me like a sensitive hipster Tarzan (but with even meatier back muscles)—I'd discover that the random dude in question was already dating someone, or wasn't into me, or wasn't straight, or thought I was gross, or all of the above.

And then I'd require a brand-new male human being to shove into the colorful rainbow-glitter world of my mind so that he might be transformed into some combination of Prince Charming, a masseur, a therapist, a breadwinner, a poet (with one surly, hormonal muse—*moi*!), and that tender young fillet of manhood with the golden locks from *The Blue Lagoon*.

It's all very Miss Piggy, this internal romantic lady world some of us cultivate. And acknowledging how stupidly boy crazy your mind is doesn't even help! You can say to yourself, "Good Jesus, why do I insist on filling up my vacuous mind with a random-dude puppet show?" But your mind will not listen to your scoldy tones. It will continue to play with its smooth-talking puppets like you never said a thing.

And it starts so young! I don't know about you, but I had the craziest, most elaborate crushes when I was in the second

grade. I was madly in love with this kid Chris—poor guy!—
and I spent basically every free second of my day picturing
us together, running through fields of flowers or swinging on
swings while holding hands (which I guess is the elementary
school version of heavy petting?). In my sad mind, Chris and I
were the perfect pair, and the whole world was our own private,
luxurious, sunshiny tampon commercial.

Do these rich imaginings only kick into overdrive in young-
ish women who feel alienated and lonely? It's easy enough
to look back and assume that my not-very-warm-and-fuzzy
family dynamics were to blame, but I don't know. I think this
boy-crazy thing is just what happens when an overactive mind
digests a steady stream of fairy tales in which the heroine is
saved from despair by a gel-haired dullard in pointy loafers.

These days, I look at my two daughters, and it kills me to
picture their little creative minds already starting to fill up with
obsessively imagined scenes starring some boy who barely
knows how to wipe his own ass yet. How do I get them to
avoid that dead-end road forever? Because when we fixate on
boys starting at a very young age, every pointless, empty interaction with a dude starts to seem powerful and electric. I don't
mean to discount the glory of hormones and attraction and
young love, but—to think of how rich and full my mind and
my heart could've been without my boy obsession! I might've
learned how to, I don't know, speak Russian, or play the piano,
or reupholster furniture!

This is the unsung glory of marriage: No more rich fucking
tapestries necessary. Time to garden, read, play guitar, cook,
write, hang out with friends, and—perhaps most importantly—
watch fifteen hours of reality TV in a row.

What I admire most about your letter is that you acknowledge that the whole crush thing is arbitrary. You hardly know
the guy in question, and your friend is hardly to blame for
deciding she likes him. We weavers aren't usually so clear-

headed. We tend to inhabit our shiny fantasy lands so completely that when someone taps us on the back and says, "It's not like that," we get confused and lash out, as if someone selfishly stole the world's only masseur-therapist-firefighter-sugar-daddy RIGHT OUT OF OUR HANDS. So pat yourself on the back right now. You may have an overactive imagination, but at least you aren't taking that out on anyone back in the real world.

I also love that you want to figure out how to redecorate your mind, to use your vivid imagination to think your way out of this. And look, I'm a big proponent of using your tapestry-weaving powers for good and not evil. But sometimes you have to let go of your shiny imaginary creations in order to give in to the magic of the real world, which is far more glorious and full of hope than it first appears. You see, the problem with weaving rich fucking tapestries is that it's like seeing one too many delightful rom-coms about soft-spoken, funny guys who say just the right thing at just the right moment. You start imagining that real-life guys never say clueless shit or smell like gorgonzola cheese. It's like training yourself, through successive wanking sessions, to only get off on redheads with giant boobs. By filling our heads with Shower Fresh–scented fantasy worlds, we not only start to expect too much but we also become easily bored with the real world and its very *real* magic. Or, we imagine that we can only exist in the real world if we fill our heads with magical distractions. We create relationships that aren't based on real compatibilities but on the crazy mixed-up tapestries that we ourselves constructed in our overactive minds.

I know I'm getting a little freaky here. What I mean is that rich tapestries block out the magic of real moments. Rich tapestries block out real people—love interests, but also other people who matter. Rich tapestries compromise friendships, and they block us from our career goals, and they blot out the sun. They train us to think that the only scene that's full color in our lives is the scene with the dude in it.

But controlling your brain is not exactly easy. You have to train yourself to romanticize a life *outside* of men and create a tapestry that's just as rich without a guy in it. That requires a kind of buoyant solitude that isn't easy to achieve.

A few things that will make your alone time more buoyant: Inspiring music. A clean space. Regular, vigorous exercise. Great books. A nice bath. A wide range of beverages in the fridge. Friendly pets. Engrossing home projects. Your setting matters! I'm not that into decorating, but you have to put a little energy into your surroundings when you live alone.

But this is also about living in the moment, isn't it? That's something we all have to learn to do, whether we're alone or not. That requires powering down all of the fantastical imagined things we'll have one day and just soaking in this moment instead. I try to ground myself several times a day and just savor what's happening right now: There are two dogs sleeping on the bed next to me. My kids in the next room are speaking in fake Italian accents. It's time to make dinner. My neck hurts. "Everyone's a building burning," Modest Mouse is singing in my ear.

The truth is, I'm not the best at this. I don't know the perfect way to make your mind into a superspecial no-boys-allowed club. But here's what I will tell my own daughters, when they start to place all of the magic outside of themselves, when they start to feel like some random dude owns the sun and the moon and the stars:

The world has told you lies about how small you are. You will look back on this time and say, "I had it all, but I didn't even know it. I was at the center, I could breathe in happiness, I could swim to the moon. I had everything I needed."

Polly

The Poisons of Materialism

Dear Polly,

I am a writer with a day job copywriting for an enormous and successful high-fashion e-commerce company. I'd resisted nailing down steady employment since graduating from university to try to stay truer to myself as a writer and artist. In the past year, I started my own magazine with my best friend—and it's doing well, considering we are funding it ourselves and resisting any content anywhere near resembling clickbait, instead providing a cohesive curation for the experimental and innovative. It's very fulfilling work, something I'm so excited to see grow. But now, this day job, while I enjoy it, is making it difficult for me to stay grounded and focused.

I've been going through phases of obsession, I imagine from being surrounded daily by luxury clothing and accessories that often cost double my monthly salary. Being surrounded by this culture brings out my impulsive side: I've overspent in moments of weakness on more occasions than I would like to count. It isn't fiscal irresponsibility I'm writing to you about, though. I could use some advice as to how not to allow my current surroundings, which are not necessarily relevant to who I am, pollute my mind this way. We're all products of our surroundings, right? Working day to day, surrounded by buyers who get allowances from the company and turn up with the latest Givenchy bag I just got paid $16 an hour to write copy about the week prior, listening to their stories of being flown to Paris for fashion week, and yet feeling on the outside of all of this in my heart of hearts—it's disorienting.

It's complicated by the fact that, although most of my close friends are also broke creative types—oh, the musicians I've dated—I really, truly like my colleagues at the fashion company. We've begun spending time together outside of work. They are good people, they are cool and all around my age, we get along well, but in the back of my mind there is this irreconcilable malaise over the discrepancy between us where priorities and lifestyle ethics are concerned. Since I've tried the starving artist thing and found *that* didn't suit me (especially not in New York, my god, the stories), and since the dream of working more meaningfully in a field like academia seems not to exist as a viable option anymore save for a lucky few, it seems I am in a good position, jobwise. But I know for a fact that there is more, and the internal struggle against being a materialistic tart without alienating my colleagues is becoming exhausting.

Help me, please, dearest Polly. I'm too much of a brooder to cope with having to sell out in order to pursue the work that is truly important to me.

Sincerely,
Wannabe Buddhist

—ɯ—

Dear Wannabe Buddhist,

The fact that you're seduced by luxury goods merely indicates that you are not a robot. A person can be turned off by the soul-sucking nature of high capitalism and still recognize, objectively, that high-end products are designed by talented artisans and luxury-branding super-geniuses who do not fuck around. Sure, maybe in the old days it was just about slapping your shitty gold logo on a bunch of moderately non-crappy handbags. Alas, like an awkward teenager who blossoms into a megalomaniacal pop star and then explodes, like a dying star, into a global lifestyle brand, the luxe-goods game is stronger than ever, having evolved from its clumsy, blingy roots into a full-service ego fuck-doll for the mega-rich.

To be clear, I don't care about these objects as signifiers of wealth and taste. My preferred look is best described as "bedraggled bag lady." What gets me, personally, is soft things. Show me a luxury item that is unbearably soft and supple, and I'll show you the electrified synapses of my brain, furiously adding and subtracting numbers in order to land in some universe where purchasing an absurd cashmere robe does not necessitate pillaging my children's college savings accounts.

You are living in the temple of temptation, WB. It is perfectly natural for you to feel like a puppet, pulled this way and that by the fickle luxe-branding overlords. That's what fickle luxe-branding overlords were born to do: make you feel weak and powerless. When you spend your days staring at bony teenagers in tall boots and touching soft things that cost more than your monthly salary, it eats away at your soul like a hungry little demon-rabbit.

But this is true of so many of the shiny distractions of our culture. Anything that temporarily fills your vision and is also delightful and tempting and gorgeous, whether it be a $5k leather jacket or a charming plate of aged cheeses or a long read on Taylor Swift befriending a wide selection of fun-loving supermodels, can derail your whole day and your values and your priorities and your identity along with it. That's just the nature of modern living. Everything is custom-designed to make us drop what we're doing and drool and feel inadequate and long for more. It's all crack, I tell you. IT'S 2016 AND THE WHOLE WORLD IS MADE OF CRACK.

When I worked full-time as a TV critic, I was regularly swept up in the heady world of pointless televised entertainments, with all of the chattering publicists and mind-numbingly bad programming that entails. Sounds harmless enough, I'm sure. But when you're swimming through hollow, crass junk every single day, it's hard not to be affected by it. Until one day you've seen one episode too many and you say to yourself, "I can't bathe in this stuff every day or I'll turn into someone I don't like."

Maybe you'll arrive at just such a breaking point eventually. But I don't think it's fair for you to consider yourself a sellout in the meantime, simply because you work for a business that makes money selling or glorifying things that people are lured into paying too much money for. Likewise, the magazine you've created might be fantastic, but there's a good chance you'll still need to negotiate with one devil or another in order to pay your bills. Sadly, becoming an adult often requires learning to negotiate with devils.

You hang out with people who like pricey stuff. That doesn't make you a materialistic tart. While it's important to honor the principles that are dear to your heart, it's also important to draw healthy boundaries between yourself and the world around you. What you do for a living doesn't have to define you. Being an idealist is worthless unless you have a strategy for sustaining yourself and aiming for a more conscientious way of living. If devil negotiation is replaced with idleness, you may not be doing business with the devil, but you may not be doing much of anything, really.

You could, instead, see your job as a daily exercise in denying the impulses you recognize as unhealthy. Or maybe you could just look at it as a way to pay the rent while you figure out what you really want from your life. Or maybe you could view it as a way to climb the editorial ladder and then leap over to a publication that supports your values. A chance to climb that ladder and rack up valuable experience is not to be trifled with. I may have been tired of covering television toward the end of my seven-year stint as a TV critic, but few other jobs would've allowed me so much time to write. I struggled to file delightful new insights every few days, like any writer does. There's something to be said for pushing past the naturally repellent aspects of any job and keeping the faith that you're picking up skills that you'll be able to use elsewhere. Even though I used to say, "I think I've learned everything I can learn here," occasionally, I don't think I would've landed in the same place if I'd only tolerated that job for two or three years. I learned to put my mixed feelings aside and meet my deadlines, week after week.

Now, as for the people you work with: You like them, but they're very different from you. Throughout life, you'll find yourself in this position. Each new job will introduce a brand-new and vastly different culture to you. It's unavoidable. I worked at an early dot-com, and the culture was pure Angry Nerds with Delusions of Grandeur. In some ways, I fit right in. But I also felt like a slow-moving herd animal among honey badgers. Pushing through that feeling was crucial; it was a dream job, and if I'd let my mournful lowing get in the way of what I actually created there, it would've been a damn shame. Likewise, when you become a parent? You are often forced to hang out with the parents of your kids' friends. For a while, I was seriously avoidant about this, but once I finally gave in and threw myself into befriending other parents, I realized what I was missing. I love those friends! They're great! If I turned my back on that crowd just because every last one of our interests and values weren't in line, my life would be far less colorful and rewarding than it is.

The bigger point: Groups can't fulfill your every need. Your spouse can't single-handedly bring you happiness. Your best female friend can't save you from being alone. Your group of college friends won't feel perfectly right for you when you're in a certain mood. There will *always* be discrepancies between you and your friends where priorities and lifestyle are concerned. So don't let it prevent you from forging new connections.

So repeat after me, WB: "I will not lose myself. I can earn money and create art, too. I can befriend Buddhists and women in $300 heels. I am not a one-dimensional, angry human with boundary issues, like those others who get so fixated on being ONE THING AND NOTHING ELSE. I contain worlds. I have many interests and many tastes, and I give zero fucks about those who question my choices. I am doing my best to build a better world around me. Everything in my life does not have to match perfectly. I like pretty things but not the materialism that sometimes comes with them. I will resist this crack-infused world and do my best to make things that matter to me. I will not lose myself."

Polly

Am I Too Weird?

Dear Polly,

I'm weird. I've always been weird. People have been calling me that since I was a child. As I exit my twenties, it has abated, but I know people still think it. They use different words for it now—"unique," "funny," "quirky," "quite a character"—but it all means the same thing: weird.

I spent a good chunk of time in college trying to be normal. I tanned, dyed my hair blond, and basically tried to look like Paris Hilton on *The Simple Life* (it was that time). I tried to wear what everyone was wearing, do what everyone was doing, say what everyone was saying. It didn't work; I was miserable. I looked the part, but I was uncomfortable around all the other normal people (girls who also looked like Paris Hilton and boys who looked like proto–*Jersey Shore* douche bags), I was so bored talking about normal things (gossip), and I was restless and lonely even when I was surrounded by people engaged in normal pursuits at normal places (clubbing, shopping, pregaming).

Eventually, I vowed to be my authentic self. No more pretending. Now, to the casual acquaintance, the professional colleague, the just-Facebook-friends friend, I'm sure I seem confident and happy just being my weird-ass self. I'm witty and sarcastic, verbose and intellectual, brazenly sexual, unabashed in my love of nerd culture, and as likely to show up in ripped jeans and a leather jacket as I am in a vintage gown. I pursue my myriad passions and hobbies with reckless abandon, and I'm never afraid to simply be different. I come off as a person who doesn't really care what other people think, and often I don't.

But when I get close to someone, the cracks in my tough exterior begin to show. To my closest friends and lovers, I show this side of myself as readily as I show my weirdness to everyone else. Some love me just as I am, but others—and especially my boyfriends—will detach or withdraw.

The crux of my problem is this: I've toned down a lot of the visual markers of my weird over the years, but as soon as you spend any time with me, it becomes pretty damn obvious. I have a massive oil painting of myself and my dog hanging in my living room next to my "stripper" pole (it's for fitness). My whole apartment is pink, covered in Hello Kitty everything, and there are framed superhero posters all over the walls. I have a closet full of costumes, wigs, and vintage clothes I've collected over the years, and my bookshelves are exploding with dense academic tomes that reside comfortably alongside my collection of sci-fi/fantasy and graphic novels. It gets worse: I still sleep with my baby blanket and a teddy bear. And this is all not to mention how I come off in conversation; I find most getting-to-know-you topics incredibly boring. I'd rather hear about your road trip to New Orleans, or the time you ran out of toilet paper while camping, or the art project you're working on in your spare time.

I used to feel proud that at last I had embraced my weird. But lately, when I bring a new person to my apartment, I feel embarrassed. I'm scared of opening myself up to someone new only to be mocked, be judged, and have the very things that make me so happy thrown back in my face like they're indicative of what's "wrong with me." It's negatively affected my ability to date. With guys I really like, I reveal too much, too soon, and I come off as crazy and/or intense, and probably more than a little insecure. They say stuff like "I'm not feeling it romantically," "I just don't see you as a girlfriend," "I think you probably like me more than I like you."

The only successful romantic relationships in my life right now are with guys I'm just hooking up with. I don't care what they think of me or if they don't think I'm "girlfriend material." We get together, we have sex, we talk, sometimes we get some food. I don't ever do relationship-y things like spend the night; I really don't want to, and they don't ask. But it makes me feel like all I'm good for is sex. Because I'm confidently weird, the "normal girl" rules don't apply to me; they don't have to worry about me having a bunch of feelings or demanding a commitment or whatever. So really, all the men I'm attracted to are either just taking advantage of my weirdness or else rejecting it.

It sucks because I want to be loved and desired FOR those things that make me different, NOT in spite of them. I would never shame someone for having interests and pursuing them. To me, a healthy, happy partnership is one where you pursue some passions as a couple, listen interestedly to those you do separately, and tolerate those you think are ridiculous. I'm really starting to think I will never find someone like that, and I will have to fake being normal in order to have a relationship where no one shames me. Polly, am I simply too weird to ever find true love?

Signed,
Weird Gal

—⟋⟍—

Dear Weird Gal,

Your assertion that you are categorically "weird" while others are categorically "normal," and that these are static qualities that can be broadcast easily with Hello Kitty decor and vintage gowns, strikes me as a little bit childish. Plenty of those Paris Hilton look-alikes and *Jersey Shore* wannabes were—*like you*—trying to figure out how to fit in (or not). They probably didn't relish every moment of sloppy dorm-room pre-gaming. And even if they did enjoy Jell-O shots and flat ironing their hair, who's to say they actually felt fulfilled while they were doing it? You assume that you are complex where others are exactly what meets the eye. But you aren't the only one who thinks that it's more interesting to hear about someone's cool road trip than to make small talk. Most people aren't that into small talk; it just happens to be the accepted opening maneuver between humans who don't know each other that well. It takes effort and a little time to achieve a real rapport.

My guess is that at least some of the shit you're taking for being out of step with the mainstream is related to your (perfectly understandable!) urge to shove all of humanity into one of two clean categories—odd and normal, vibrant and dullsville, unique and average.

Your taste for reductive dichotomies, along with your outsized reactions to other people's perceptions of you, may not always serve you, but they probably spring forth from your sensitivity and smarts. You're quick to pick up on ambivalence. You're quick to turn this evidence over and over in your mind. You're quick to make meaning from these messages. And you feel like you need to explain your choices, to react, to *do* something to make the whole picture clearer and more palatable to other people.

But you don't! You don't have to explain a goddamn thing—to anyone, ever! All you really need, more than anything else, is the ability to tolerate the fact that some people are going to like you, some people are going to dislike you, some people are going to hate you, and—yes!—some people are going to drop to their knees and say, "SMART, UNPREDICTABLE, SENSITIVE, UNIQUE WOMAN, WHERE HAVE YOU BEEN ALL MY LIFE?"

But first, you're going to need to relax your grip on your worldview a little and accept yourself for who you are once and for all. And while you're at it, accept that the so-called ultra-normals out there are far more complex than you give them credit for. The only enemy you have right now is you. You're casting a wide net and meeting a wide range of people. That's great, but listen to me: Anyone under the sun could feel unnerved by that process. Anyone. Meeting new people and showing them who you are and maybe even making out with them? That's an inherently shaky, uncertain experience! It's almost impossible not to present a blustery, overconfident version of yourself in those circumstances and to form angry, defensive impressions from your bad experiences. After enough bad interactions, your bluster and confidence start to give way to self-doubt.

And that wouldn't be so bad, but you are a truth teller! You're a confessional person by nature. If there's a feeling of doubt in the room, you have to acknowledge it, put it into words, bring it to light.

But sometimes we confessional overthinkers have to bite our tongues. Sometimes we have to remind ourselves that it's not necessary to DO anything. We can just stay present and listen. We can watch and observe. Even when we know that someone thinks we're flawed and strange and out of step with what's considered "normal," we can remain silent. I regularly ask my husband to vet my more long-winded or confrontational e-mails. "You don't have to say all of this stuff," he usually tells me. He points out that in professional settings, when a conflict arises, most people just act unconcerned and faintly unaware. They don't go into detail. They are polite but brief.

"Unconcerned" and "faintly unaware"! These words have never been used to describe me. This goes against everything I stand for, everything I live for, everything I am! I am *concerned* and *aware*. I notice things, and when I notice them, I say so. I cannot let tiny things drop. I refuse! I am a blaring siren! "Do you see what I'm seeing?" I ask over and over again.

Ah, but people hate that, Weird Gal. They really do. So many people are allergic to confessional, outspoken women. And let's face it, we're not always serving the common good. We're neurotic motherfuckers with way too much on our minds at all times.

So here's what we have to do: We have to be self-protective but still vulnerable. Does that sound impossible? Sometimes it is. But here's how it works: You don't put yourself in situations where you're going to cycle through bluster and neediness. That means you really can't hook up with random men. Even if you never let down your guard in those situations, they still hurt you. They fuck with your sense of yourself. They lead you to believe you're only good for sex, and you can't EVER settle for feeling that way.

You have to protect yourself from yourself, too. You can open your heart and tell the truth to your trusted friends. That's good for you. But don't tell yourself that you're confident enough to share yourself with just anyone. Don't open up to people who don't understand and accept you yet. Wait until you feel completely comfortable.

I know you claim that you're already careful about this, but I don't buy it. You sound conflicted to me. You say you're never afraid to be different, but then you ask me if you're too different. You say you feel totally confident about being weird, but then you ask if you're too weird for love. You say you're brazenly sexual, but then you say you want more than these one-night stands you're having. As long as you're conflicted, no one else will be comfortable with you. As much as you might say, "I'm proud of who I am, damn it!" your statements about yourself still sound like marketing copy.

Likewise: You put a stripper pole in your living room, and when people ask about it, you say, "It's for fitness." That's like

saying you buy *Playboy* for the articles. Yes, it's possible that
you discovered along the way that *Playboy* had good articles
and that a stripper pole gets you fit. But there's a reason you
picked up a copy of *Playboy* over *Vanity Fair,* or picked out a
stripper pole instead of, say, a set of kettlebells. When you're
defensive about your choices, that makes other people less
accepting of those choices, too.

It's not a problem for the men who just want to sleep with
you, because they *want* to keep their distance. But for guys
who could be genuinely interested in you, defensiveness and
bravado that conceal larger insecurities add up to a major red
flag. These things say, "I may pretend not to care about what
you think, but I actually care *a lot.* I want to explain myself, but
I shouldn't have to explain myself." You're wearing a sign that
says, "HERE'S WHO I AM, GODDAMN IT. LOVE ME OR
SCREW YOU," and handing out cards that say, "How would
you rate me on a scale of 1 to 10, where 10 means 'strongly
approve' and 1 means 'Get out of my face, freak!' "

It's time to take better care of yourself, to embrace and support yourself more, to remind yourself what you truly care
about, and to make better judgments about who is worthy of
the full, glorious light of weirdness you will someday shine on
the world, far and wide.

And you will! Oh, will you shine! I love that you know what
you like and don't like, that you show yourself to the world no
matter what, that you sleep with a baby blanket and a bear. You
do what you like, even when you don't feel appreciated for it.
Don't lose that.

But you do have to recognize that people like you—and me,
and lots of people out there—will always feel some tension
between themselves and the world. We're tempted to provoke,
to deliberately rub people the wrong way. We do this because
we're pissed that the world isn't kind to us. We're sick of being

treated badly just because we have unusual preferences and strong opinions and we talk a little too much. It's easier to go against the grain if you're thick-skinned, but we're not. We're sensitive. And nothing is quite as hard as being a sensitive, aggressive weirdo.

It gets easier when you surrender a little, when you let down your defenses. It gets easier when you allow yourself to be vulnerable. You don't have to make a pitch. You can tell the truth. "I got the pole in a stripper-obsessed phase, and now I just use it for fitness." "I'm kind of a strange person and I like what I like, but sometimes it's hard to be me." "I used to be sure of exactly who I was. Now I'm more confused about it."

I think you're in the middle of a transition. Some of your choices make sense to you, and others feel outdated. Wear THAT on your sleeve. Resist the urge to reveal every inch of yourself—or to invite people to your place—immediately. Let them get to know you gradually. Practice sitting still in the presence of someone whose disappointment and lack of interest are becoming palpable. Sit with it instead of trying to convince them otherwise. Sit with it instead of getting defensive or angry. Practice saying, "I'm opinionated. I'm a weirdo. I'm not for everyone."

You're trotting out all your secrets right now. You can't do that until you feel good about your secrets and you accept that lots of people won't like you once they know who you are. That's true for anyone.

A lot of people won't be into you. You will feel the pain of that for your entire life, trust me. You really should accept it and learn to deal with it—not by shutting people out or becoming defensive or rigid, but by (paradoxically!) allowing people space to feel however they happen to feel and making small adjustments to how you move through the world based on what feels good and what doesn't.

It's okay to be an oversensitive freak. Oversensitive freaks tend to overreact. They tend to spin in circles. But they are some of the most loyal, interesting, intense people around, and they just get better as they age. Welcome to the tribe!

Polly

Crushed by an STD

Dear Polly,

I had a devastating breakup earlier this year. In the aftermath, I tried to take care of myself: I exercised. I ate healthier. I traveled. I spent time with friends and family. I threw myself into work projects. I started seeing a therapist. I even went on a few promising (and not-so-promising) dates.

A few months after the breakup, just when I was starting to feel human again, I got very drunk and had unprotected sex with a good friend. The lack of protection was obviously a mistake; I've always been vigilant about condom usage and both of us are regularly tested for STDs, and we both acknowledged our error in judgment. Several days later, I developed two sores on my genitals and immediately went to see my doctor the next day. She visually diagnosed me with herpes, which a blood test later confirmed. I sobbed in her office, and I've cried every day since.

My doctor has been absolutely exemplary and understanding in terms of answering questions and providing comfort; I feel very grateful to have her as my physician. My friend who I slept with has also been wonderful; I informed him right away. He was concerned but listened with an open mind and heart and was deeply reassuring. I know that while it's not curable, it is treatable and that the stigma and shame are the hardest parts to manage. I know that even if we had used protection, I still would've been at risk since it's transmitted via skin-to-skin contact. I know it's possible for herpes to lay dormant for years without showing symptoms (either of us could've contracted it previously) and the only way to truly protect yourself against STDs is to abstain from sex.

I know all of this. I keep repeating it to myself like a mantra. But I can't shake the feeling that I've massively, massively fucked up, and it feels like this diagnosis is confirming every long-held negative thought I've ever had about myself, mostly about how I'm a reckless, selfish drunk who's unworthy of love.

It had been so hard to stay hopeful and authentic and vulnerable these last few months, but I was so proud of myself for taking positive, active steps to better myself and live the life I always wanted. Now, with this development, the idea of putting myself out there and ever trying to date again feels daunting, terrifying, and impossible. I even feel myself starting to withdraw from the life that I rebuilt: I'm bailing on social plans, I canceled an upcoming trip to see friends, I've lost interest in the job I love and worked years to get. I'm falling apart because I just can't let go of the idea that this was supposed to be the good part. I worked so hard, I took care of myself, I tried to be considerate of others, and I still messed it all up, and I now have to live with the consequences. I'm depressed and angry and crushed.

I'm seeing a new therapist. (My previous therapist left the practice one month before this happened.) I'm taking a long, possibly permanent, hiatus from drinking. My doctor is tremendous. The two people I've confided in (the previously mentioned friend and my best female friend) have been wildly supportive. But how do I navigate this for the rest of my life? I know I'm going to meet people who will judge me, and I don't know how to navigate those responses without crumbling. I know a genital herpes diagnosis is not the end of the world, but why does it still feel that way?

Crushed

—m—

Dear Crushed,

You feel like your diagnosis is the end of the world because it IS the end of a world that you inhabited for a long time. And somehow this feels like your fault. It feels like something that will plague you forever. You feel like you'll never get over the stigma of this. You think that anyone you have feelings for will cringe and run away, and that behavior will only confirm your darkest fears: that you're fucked-up and selfish and unworthy of love.

This situation plays on your worst insecurities. You already felt like a reckless drunk before, as you explained, and now you have what feels like an outward manifestation of that fact.

But you were going to have to deal with the fact that you felt like a reckless, selfish drunk who's unworthy of love *either way*. This situation forces you to deal with it now, all at once. Instead of tripping along and making mistakes and eventually waking up to how little you like your bad habits, this diagnosis is making you face them immediately.

And even though it's easy to say to yourself, "I got herpes because I massively, massively fucked up," plenty of people get herpes without fucking up at all. Their boyfriend or girlfriend or spouse gave it to them. They used protection with someone they trusted, and they still got it. They got it, and they couldn't fathom how they got it. Imagine being a gay man in the early '80s dying a slow, horrible death and thinking that it happened because you fucked up. Imagine being told by a parent, by a priest, that you're dying BECAUSE YOU MADE BAD CHOICES.

It wasn't true for them, and it isn't true for you. You have to deny these voices in your head when you hear them. You have to stand up for yourself, to yourself, and say, *"I am NOT being punished for being a reckless drunk."* This world is filled with reckless, selfish people who are reckless and selfish in ways that are horribly damaging and hideous and unfair. The guy who sold me the house where I now live, a guy who had a wife and two kids, was killed in a head-on collision last year by some fucked-up teenager who seemed to think that driving was just like playing a really exciting video game. Getting wasted and sleeping with a friend without protection isn't the most cautious thing in the world, but on the scale of fuckups available to humankind it's a small one.

No one with a brain in their heads will look at that kind of a mistake and think, "Boy, are you a fuckup." No one with any sense will hear that you have herpes and think, "Jesus, what a wreck. No thank you." People who think these kinds of things are beneath you. They are stigmatizing you to sustain a belief that nothing terrible will ever happen to them. It's a common response. There are people who treat cancer patients like they must've turned down breast milk for blue Slurpees as babies, or they must've spent their teenage years sunbathing while huffing spray paint. There are people who treat divorced women like they must've gained too much weight or henpecked their poor innocent husbands to death. These are the dots we connect in order to assure ourselves that nothing bad will ever happen to us.

You don't have a debilitating illness or a death sentence. You don't have something that will prevent you from loving or being loved. You don't have a hopeless, lonely future. What you do have now is a really efficient, effective litmus test for future sexual partners and friends. You have a reason to treat yourself with respect, to not get drunk and reckless. You have a reason *not* to just hop into bed with someone without talking it over first.

This herpes thing is a giant drag. I get that. It sucks. But if anything, it proves that you are *not* a selfish, reckless drunk. Because if you were, you wouldn't be taking a hard look at your life right now and talking openly about it with your friend. You wouldn't be preparing for a new life, in which you have to have a pretty serious conversation with anyone you're going to fool around with. Your emotional response to this situation isn't just a response to the situation itself; it's also a response to the commitments you're now taking on: to face this, to talk to people about it, to tell future partners about it, to navigate this new reality with your eyes open. Do you know how many people don't have the nerve to do those things? If you were selfish and reckless, you'd deal with this upsetting situation by drinking and escaping and avoiding everything. You're not doing that.

I was a pretty reckless drunk for a while, a fact I wasn't remotely willing to face until my dad died when I was twenty-five years old. His death helped to shake me out of a pretty dramatic downward spiral. Without that event, I might've languished in confusion and self-hatred for a long time. That awful time snapped me out of a lot of my bad habits.

Now you have an awful time to get through. You'll have to live in a new way. You'll have to face yourself and overcome some of your unhealthy tendencies.

Talk to anyone living with herpes (and there are plenty of them around you whether you know it or not), and they'll tell you that it's really hard at first, but it gets easier, and the affliction itself gets less dramatic. Even though you can never completely forget about it, it doesn't end up being the giant scarlet letter on your chest that you imagine it will be at first.

Whatever you do, don't continue to cut yourself off from others. Don't let your shame take over. Shame and suspicions that you're fundamentally unlovable: These things may be kicked up by a herpes diagnosis, but they were there all along, asking you to address them. So keep addressing them, *but separate them from the STD itself.* The STD is an unfortunate thing that happened to you, nothing more and nothing less. It doesn't have to carry all of this weight if you don't let it. So be strong and separate it from the rest of your issues. File it under "Unfortunate Things That Happened."

You are just a person with regular flaws, fumbling your way toward a satisfying life. You've been handed a big challenge, but one that's going to help you to grow up and take care of yourself and connect honestly with other people. You don't have to love this challenge right now. You can cry every day and feel terrible about it. But this challenge wasn't meant to topple everything else you're doing that's good in your life. This challenge fits right in with your exercising and eating healthier and traveling and connecting with friends and taking care of yourself. This is you, facing whatever comes next while also acknowledging that you've been thrown for a loop. In the months after my dad's death, I could see that I would have to become a new kind of person in order to survive. I felt terrible, of course, but you can feel terrible and also feel fully alive. You can feel crushed and also feel inspired and hopeful. In your darkest moments, look for some hope. It's there.

You aren't alone. This isn't the end of the world, not even close. When you look back on the Days Before Herpes, you'll say, "I was more careless, but not nearly as happy back then. I take care of myself now, and I'm more protective of my heart, and my life is so much better." You feel ashamed now, but that shame isn't going to stick around for long. You're going to learn how to roll your eyes at other people's judgment.

You know who else has to learn how to do that? Every person on the planet. And if you keep facing these feelings, shame and the idiotic judgments of others won't have much power over you. You won't be crumbling and depressed. You'll be clear about who you are. You'll know what you will and won't stand for. You'll be stronger than ever. People who stand up for themselves are magnetic—partly because most people don't.

Whether or not you can feel it yet, you've just joined us

here, where the once broken and the shamed and the damaged stand together and say, "Other people's ignorance and casual rejection don't define me. I know who I am."

I KNOW WHO I AM. Repeat those words every morning, okay? I know who I am. I am honest and brave and stronger than ever.

Polly

II

You Are Uniquely Qualified to Bring You the World

What Would Kanye Do?

Polly,

My question is a simple and boring one: How do I find love? And, more importantly, how do I cultivate self-esteem? I'm in my late twenties, and I tend to get into relationships with dudes who are only half-interested in me, and then I badger them to death about their half-assed interest until the relationship slowly dies. What I want most, MOST, in the world is a happy family. Children I feel joy with. A genuinely happy marriage that lasts until I kick the goddamn bucket. I grew up with very unhappy, miserable parents who immigrated to the States, and I don't even know what to look for in a partner or a relationship. I feel like if a guy is "nice" (i.e., doesn't hit me or call me names and has generally good character), then I should just quit whining and wondering about why they're not crazy about me, why they never pursue me, why they are always so goddamn tepid.

I want a big, passionate, happy, funny, fun love. I am afraid I will never find it. I think I am as likable as the next person, but I'm not sure how to make myself attractive to men. I guess I just feel ugly and unlovable, and I would like to stop.

I love your advice. (Is straight-up "I love you" too much? Probably, but still, I do!) I've been reading your stuff for a couple years on *Rabbit Blog,* and now I stalk you on *The Awl.*

Thanks,
A Reader

—ᴍ—

Dear Reader,

I love you, too, mostly because (1) you love me already, (2) you've put in a little effort to follow me here, (3) I can relate to wanting for years to tear my hair out over tepid mother-fuckers, and (4) when you ask me this very simple question, I feel like a mathematical genius or a historian whose thoughts separate into layers and then keep expanding to infinity so that I don't know where to start because there are just so many possibilities, all of them rich and exciting. And even though a regular person who didn't love me and didn't follow me here and isn't frustrated over tepid motherfuckers will read that and say, "Jesus, lady, you're an advice columnist, not a fucking math genius or historian, and even if you have fifty million approaches to this woman's totally mundane fixations, that hardly qualifies you as one of today's great minds. I'm sure she creeps men out because she's boring or her ass is enormous. And you're creepy, too, because you're fucking old and you're still dedicating all of this time to twentysomething girl trouble when you could maybe be doing something vaguely worthwhile with your life, if you weren't so smug about your pathetic little Interwebs hobby."

See how it works? You dig me, you put in effort, you aren't remotely tepid, we can relate to each other, and you make me feel like the things that are patently fucked about me are actually thrilling and vital and they somehow matter. (And I know you're exciting, and I love your juicy booty, but that's not the point.)

Now imagine for a second that someone were to write to me and say, "Look, you're just okay and you're old and you're wasting your time on this bullshit." And imagine that I spend several hours of my time explaining why I'm awesome and my work here is incredibly significant to the health of the planet, and I fucking matter and I have great ideas, brilliant fucking ideas, I'm a genius, and seriously, what the fuck is wrong with you? Suddenly this tepid bit of flotsam is taking up my time, and instead of turning away from it, I'm making claims that my work is deeply important (which I realize is a highly subjective stance).

I'm starting to sound just like Kanye.

I love Kanye, and he sounds the way he sounds in interviews for a very good reason. He sounds that way because he's an artist with great ideas who not only lives in a racist world but also lives in a world that isn't all that appreciative of someone who delivers a passionate, angry response to his critics. He lives in a world that devalues free-flowing, emotional discourse from a black man unless it's packaged very neatly into a rap. (Please note: This world also devalues free-flowing, emotional discourse from a woman unless she's also funny AND sexy. If you're not super fucking hot and funny, you can go fuck yourself, ladies.)

Kanye isn't perfect, but you pretty much either love him and think he's a genius and then he makes some sense to you, or you don't get it and he seems crazy. Maybe you don't love him because you don't love his music or some of the mistakes he's made in the past, or maybe you don't love him because you're a racist; those two responses actually look the same to him, and why shouldn't they? Because the world is, verifiably, filled with racist motherfuckers, this is not a confused response. It's an emotional one. He doesn't love you either way. Maybe it's a mistake for him to keep talking about it. Or maybe he's helping everyone by being the symbol of a kind of anger that people are vexed by and afraid of. All I know is, I feel for him. Because lots of people don't understand what he's doing, and so they belittle him. And he's right, they DO just want to meet him, leech off him, take photos of him, point at him, get him to sign some deal, kiss his ass, and laugh behind his back.

To which he says, "Fuck you AND your Hampton house, I'll fuck your Hampton spouse, came on her Hampton blouse," etc.

I know, add misogyny to my ass-objectification. Look, I have to be my brutal self, too. This is the texture of the world we live in, and stepping around it politely makes me feel crazy.

So here's where we land: You need to tell tepid to fuck right off, Kanye-style. If you vow right now that the second you see tepid, you're going to back up and say, "No fucking thanks," and move on without looking back, then your self-esteem will immediately bounce back from years of abuse. That means retiring the soliloquy about how great you are. That means no more badgering. Replace the badgering with a rap. Write it down, file it away, move the fuck on. (*Fuck you AND your futon. I'll fuck your best friend, Sean. I'll fuck him till the dawn. I'll make your man my pawn. Fuck having late-night drinks. Fuck playing tiddlywinks. Fuck all your tepid kinks. Your half-assed shit still stinks.*)

And you know what? Okay, I'm stretching this Kanye metaphor beyond the breaking point, but bear with me. We live in some crazy fucking times. Sexism is everywhere, and we're not even confused by it anymore; we're just drinking it down like water without thinking. How can we make enemies of people we want to get dirty with, and get love from, and make babies with?

And men are great, let's be honest. Those filthy, simple-minded, government-bungling ball scratchers. We love those dicks. Love. Sincerely, desperately, quietly, devotedly. I have one in my own home—in my bed, of all places. Who let him in here? But he's great, really—much more honorable and kinder than me, as a matter of fact. Sharp as a tack and best all around.

But here's a little anecdote for you: I went out to a bar the other night with some women, and it was late at night

(I have two kids; this is rare for me), and there were some men there—regular guys, reasonably okay-looking. Flirtatious high-fiving types? And they started shooting the shit with us. And we women were polite. Some were nice; others ignored them. Well, I like a high fiver. I spent years around the sports-loving bro species, and I appreciate them. That said, I don't want to follow their meandering bullshit wherever it leads, and I don't want to flirt, and I don't want to feed their egos. I want to engage in a give-and-take conversation while occasionally calling them on their shit.

But you know what? It's an accident of fate that I ever hung out with high fivers in my entire life because most of those guys hate me. HATE. They find me physically repellent.

These particular guys, I couldn't care less about. But that's the soup I've been in, without knowing it, since I was really young and single. Most guys I met preferred my flirty lady friends to me. Now sometimes slightly weird guys, slightly smarter, stranger, maybe more damaged, or maybe just more sensitive guys (or both), they were a little intrigued by my not-buying-it face and my assertive here's-what-I-fucking-think fat mouth, or maybe they just liked my ass, which truly was a force of nature for a time. So what was it, my ass or my big personality? My sorta-pretty face, or my almost-smart words? I never knew. UNTIL THE BITCHES GOT TEPID. And by then we were already sleeping together and hanging out around the clock.

But did I say to myself, "Oh. He doesn't like me. He likes my ass. A lot. Enough to put up with my bullshit for a while"? No. I didn't say that. I can look back now and see the truth. "That dude didn't even like me." Or: "That dude didn't even like women all that much." Or: "He liked my personality enough to date me, but he would've liked me a lot more if I were about half as smart and half as talkative."

And remember about Kanye? Remember your badgering? When you suspect that a guy doesn't like you? You talk too much. Instead of talking so much, you should be saying, "Fuck you AND your Hampton house." Yes, your first priority should be to keep an open mind, to listen, to observe men with a clear, uncluttered perspective. Your second priority should be to never, ever waste a minute of your time on a guy who's tepid.

Because tepid is everywhere. Tepid is the air we breathe. Listen to me: We women can't do anything right. We can't say what we mean, we can't be ourselves, we can't age, we can't talk about feelings, we can't fuck up. This is how it feels to be a woman, motherfucker. The world is filled with human beings who want us to shut up and shake our asses—the end.

Can you fucking imagine if we had our own Kanye? For her to have Kanye's power, and get invited to do the late-night circuit, of course she'd have to be a mega-hot, funny-as-shit woman who walked around looking exactly like the chick in the short skirt who eats giant hamburgers on those Carl's Jr. ads, but instead of eating a hamburger, she'd be saying, "FUCK YOU, YOU ARE A SEXIST FUCK." I mean, sure, we have our women who look mortal and say this. Are they on TV? Rachel Maddow, she's on TV. How many people in that bar would even know who the fuck she is? Who listens closely to Lena Dunham (who *is* gorgeous by the way)? No, she's not shaped right to listen to, right? She's too full of herself? She's too annoying?

Let's not fall down that rabbit hole. All I'm saying is, here we are in a fucked-up world. And even when you find your species, you still are sometimes just a piece of ass to the best of them. Not even because they're incredibly sexist—maybe they're just pragmatic, or ambivalent in this case. They don't happen to love you, is all. They don't think you're a math genius or a historian. They think that when you talk, you're wasting their time a little. That doesn't mean they're bad. Sure, you want those guys and their futons and their best friend, Sean, to go fuck themselves, but that doesn't mean they're evil. But once they don't love you, who the fuck cares about them? Were those dudes in the bar sexist for not being into me, or did they just think I was sort of bossy and repellent? Who the fuck cares?

You're hunting a very small group, that's all. Your target demographic, it's small. There's more than one of them, but they're not everywhere.

That doesn't mean your odds are bad! You will find love. Believe me. But in order to find it, I think you have to prepare yourself for a life alone and be at peace with that. It's a real tightrope walk. I get it. But you won't tell tepid to fuck off if you don't believe in your heart that you will rock it out one way or another.

In order to tell tepid to fuck off once and for all, you MUST recognize that life among those who don't appreciate or under-stand you is bullshit. You don't want to live that way. You don't want to be badgery and lonely while you're with someone. You'd rather be alone.

What will make ALONE look good to you? You have to work on that. Because single life needs to look really, really good. You have to believe in it if you're going to hold out for that rare guy who makes you feel like all of your ideas start rapidly expanding and approaching infinity when you talk to him. You need to have a vision of life alone, stretching into the future, and you need to think about how to make that vision rich and full and pretty. You have to put on an artist's mind-set and get creative and paint a portrait of yourself alone that's breathtak-ing. You have to bring the full force of who you are and what you love to that project.

And then you go out into the world with an open heart, and you let people into your life, and you listen, and you embrace them for who they are. You make new friends. You do new things that make you feel more like the strong single woman who owns the world that's in your vision. And you don't sleep with anyone until things are much warmer than lukewarm. And you accept that if things are lukewarm after that, you will be forced to kick a motherfucker to the curb, but with kindness, with forgiveness.

You have to do a lot. And you have to do it all against a backdrop of indifference that, as you get older, curdles into a kind of disgust. But you know what? We have each other. We have worlds within us, you and me. This mean, mean planet still rewards those who can see the depth and beauty of what they carry around inside of themselves. This indifferent landscape will rise up and give you love if you share what you have inside, if you dare to believe in your potential even as people tell you it's a mirage, if you ignore the ones who are allergic to free-flowing, emotional discourse from you. They are everywhere, and they don't matter. God bless them. Come on their Hampton blouse, and move on.

Polly

My Boyfriend Has Never Had a Job

Hi, Polly,

My boyfriend and I have been dating for three and a half years. We met in college, which is like an incubator for relationships: You look for smart, funny, liberal (if you're in the South) partners. The notion of "Is this person practical?" doesn't really register.

All right, I'll cut to the chase: My boyfriend is chronically unemployed, and I can't decide whether to break up with him or if even thinking that makes me a shallow, awful person.

He's never had a job during our entire relationship. Part of that was time spent in college, which doesn't count. But then he graduated with a useless humanities degree and couldn't find a job. I graduated with the same degree, but considering I've had to work my ass off since I was seventeen to survive, I hustled and found work.

I'm currently in graduate school, pursuing my dreams, but I still pay our entire rent. It's so much stress. And he knows it—he does all of the housework; I know he tries to find jobs (he's just not good at it?). I think he's clinically depressed, but considering we have no money, it's not like he can get treatment for it.

At what point does a total lack of practicality become a deal breaker? I love him, he's my best friend, our cats like him more than me. But I feel more like his parent than his girlfriend. And there's a part of me that wonders, if I break up with him, what will he *do*? I worry that he'd have to move back in with his emotionally unavailable parents, sink into a deeper depression . . . Sigh.

Help.

Signed,
Freeloader Lover

—m—

Dear Freeloader Lover,

The words "chronically unemployed" imply that your boyfriend *has* been employed at some point. But if he's twenty-five or twenty-six years old and he hasn't had a job since college or before that, he isn't chronically unemployed. HE IS STUCK.

You have to dump him. For your sake, but also for his. He's not going to get unstuck until he takes responsibility for himself, walks out the door, and gets some kind of a job. Any job. The way he's living right now is unacceptable. I don't care if he's looked for work before and can't find what he wants. He can work *somewhere*. He can do SOMETHING. You don't need a housekeeper. You need a partner.

And here's what you need to understand, more than anything else: *You aren't helping him by paying for everything.* You're hurting him. He's like an addict. He's needy and he depends on you and he's hiding from his whole life. He thinks that he can feed the cats and do all the housework and maybe he can hide from the world forever.

He's wrong. And more than that, hiding isn't making him happy. He feels like a loser. He feels like it's only a matter of time before you dump him. These aren't good feelings. I've been in that state before, and if I had someone who loved me, who was willing to pay ALL of the rent when I was young and sad and didn't want to do anything with myself, I would've taken full advantage of that. Thank god I didn't have that person in my life.

I've also felt like someone's parent before. I know how you feel, and it sucks. You feel responsible for holding this grown adult together. But it can also feel good, in a weird way. It's satisfying to be needed that much, especially if you've never been needed before. It can bring out all of your nurturing instincts, whether you're a man or a woman. If you walk in the door and there's someone there, happy to see you, cooking you dinner, thrilled to hear about your day? That can be pretty satisfying. Some of us have never had that. And if he gives you a lot of credit for being someone who knows how to go out into the real world and bring home the bacon? Well, it's hard not to take pride in that.

The problem is that nine times out of ten it doesn't last. Not only do finances become strained to the point where you can't do anything out of the house, ever, but those excellent dinners disappear. Instead of being greeted with a smile, you're greeted with the sound of snoring on the couch. Or the sound of a bong being fired up while *Assassin's Creed* loads on the TV. If your guy doesn't already smoke a lot of pot . . . well, I'm sort of guessing he does. But he has a big problem either way.

And that means you've got a big problem.

I get how hard it is to dump someone you feel 100 percent responsible for. When I was in my late twenties, I had what I thought was a really great boyfriend who in reality wasn't bringing much to the table and couldn't face the real world. We were stuck in a bubble together. He was childlike. He could be great company sometimes, but he wasn't a great partner yet. He needed to grow up.

I will never forget watching him walk away after I broke up with him. He looked like a sad little kid. I felt like I'd just kicked my own son out of the house. I know that sounds absurd, but really it was that crushing. I didn't just feel guilty;

I felt completely heartbroken and ill. I wanted my kid back. I wanted him to feel safe.

And I didn't get over him quickly, either. I wanted to date adult men, but I still wanted my ex in my life, because I loved him so much. I wanted to take him with me wherever I went, like a teddy bear. I never wanted to say good-bye. He understood me. It was so comfortable and comforting! He really loved me—and, again, HE NEEDED ME.

But you know what we both needed? To break our codependent bond and face ourselves. That wasn't going to happen when we were together. So he was a casualty of my youth. And I didn't find someone who was the same intellectual match for me for years after that. I fell in love, but I didn't feel that comforted and loved again until I met my husband.

You will feel lonely and sad. You'll miss your boyfriend. But you have to push him out the door. You can't be responsible for where he lands. You could give him a month to find a job. But honestly, I think you already know that he needs to live alone regardless. He needs to handle his own life. He needs to grow up. He's not going to do that living with you. He's depressed, and he wants you to take care of him. Taking care of him doesn't help him; it only makes him more depressed.

He'll need to get a job and an apartment and learn to fend for himself. But you might be surprised at how independent he can become, once he's forced to snap out of it. He might hate working an entry-level job (who doesn't?), but he'll be better off for it. If he wants to crawl back to his family's house, that's his call. But you have to remind yourself that it's not your problem.

Struggling with a shitty job is part of growing up. You punch the clock at a horrible job for a few years, and guess what? It sucks. But eventually, you start to figure out how to get a job you actually enjoy. That doesn't happen when you're vacuuming and playing with cats full-time.

Let your boyfriend down gently. Doing that doesn't make you a shallow, awful person. It makes you a sane person. It means you care about his well-being. Don't blame him for being lost and paralyzed by his circumstances. Tell him you believe in him, but you need to move forward separately now. Dump him with compassion. But dump him. He'll thank you for it someday.

Polly

Devil Town

Dear Polly,

Two years ago, I was sexually assaulted by a longtime pal. We'd worked together for a decade, shared triumphs and losses over the years, and I considered him one of my most trustworthy friends. And then he hit some especially rough patches— alcoholism, midlife-crisis kind of stuff. He left his wife, ignored his child, and went off the deep end, constantly partying and living up this new single life. He also became so aggressive toward women that he was banned from our usual drinking establishment. Although he was popular with a particularly hip, snarky, creative subset of people in our small town, he was also widely disliked, in large part because women tend to be creeped out by him. For many years, I defended him, excusing the weird vibes others perceived as his "dumb sense of humor." Turns out, those folks called it. I'd already started edging away from him, but given our long history, untangling from our friendship wasn't easy. And then one night he attacked me at a club, repeatedly and violently shoving his hands under my dress, grabbing between my legs, all while laughing in my face as I tried to shove him away. If it had been anyone else, I'd have grabbed security, called the cops, pressed charges. As it was, I had to run to my car to get away from him.

The next day, he shrugged it off but agreed it would be best that I moved out of our shared work space. My husband was appalled (obviously), but being aware of the hell this guy's wife and child were already going through, we decided it would be best to move on without adding to their suffering (by pressing charges or otherwise confronting him). By this point, many people in town had a horror story about dealing with him as he was constantly drunk, starting fights, torpedoing his business, and otherwise burning all bridges. Eventually, he ran out of people willing to associate with him. He also got a DUI. That must have been a wake-up call, because after that he started laying low and even convinced his wife to take him back. Several months passed, then he reemerged on the scene, getting a job at a place where I did consulting work and popping up at social engagements. I found myself reacting with both uncontrollable anxiety and disgust that he would get to be the cool kid again after hurting so many people. I started sharing what had happened—and how much I was struggling over being confronted with him—with mutual friends. To my great relief, they were horrified and quite clear in their desire to support me. I was especially gratified that my guy friends took this so seriously.

Except for two of them. These two not only celebrated his return but actively campaigned for him, helping him get a really good job and inviting him into our shared circle. This put me—and the friends supporting me—into a terrible position. It's too small a town to easily shun someone, but if it weren't for the efforts of these two guys, at least my closest circle would have been safe.

I basically lost my shit over this. How could they be on his side and not take what happened seriously? How could they advocate for someone who sexually assaulted me and others? They're supposed to be my friends. When one of them got screwed over by his boss years ago, I took a public stand against the business, despite doing so having an impact on my own career. I've been there for the other one more times than I can remember. And they're jettisoning all that for the sake of this creep, whom I know better than either of them?

Eventually, they started to consider *me* the asshole for making them feel bad about supporting a man who was, in their words, "trying to rebuild his life." I realized that I was going to have to give up this battle. So, deep breath, we had some conversations in which I conveyed my intent to agree to disagree.

Then, a couple nights ago, I was fixing something on my husband's Facebook page and saw an interaction in the side feed between one of those two friends and the guy who assaulted me. I lost my shit all over again, chatted angrily at him, to which he responded horribly, accusing me of focusing my anger at him instead of the person I "think" hurt me, saying I'm awful for not forgiving, etc. So now I'm mad at myself because I already knew they talked all the time, plus I made a point of deciding to at least forgive the two guys for not understanding. Now I've reneged on that promise. I'm finally really the bad guy.

I need help figuring out how to forgive. Am I crazy for thinking my friends should be loyal to me over someone who has behaved so horribly? Other than moving away (not currently an option), how do I navigate this? Do I just pretend things are fine until maybe eventually they will be? Why don't these people understand? Why do I have to suck it up and the guy who attacked people gets to skate? Why does the bad guy get to win? Am I being overly judgmental, forgetting that I, too, can be a real jerk at times? (I have never assaulted anyone, please note.) Do I want too much? I've been asking myself these questions for months. I'm stuck.

Floundering

—cw—

Dear Floundering,

Your letter reminds me of a Daniel Johnston song called "Devil Town." Johnston tells the story of living in an evil place without knowing it, only to wake up one morning and discover that all of his friends are vampires. "Oh lord, it really brings me down about the devil town," he sings.

It's such a strange, simple song, but it's also devastatingly sad. You think you're surrounded by trustworthy friends, and then you wake up one morning and realize they can't be trusted.

Some readers might believe that you're overreacting to your situation. To me, the crucial part of your story is not the grabbing, per se, but the fact that this guy laughed in your face as you said no. That's malice. It suggests not only that he's a deeply screwed-up person but also that he's intent on making other people feel powerless. That malice is what makes it almost impossible for you to get over this. He was your friend, and suddenly he wanted to torment you.

On top of that, it sounds like he never apologized. He shrugged it off, apparently never owned up to his other aggressive acts, and never addressed this insane, predatory behavior that cropped up in the midst of his drinking. If that's true and he never faced what he did, then basically he's the same dangerous asshole he always was. He did not reform himself. He is still a bad guy. It's disturbing that your friends can't see that. But it's also not all that surprising.

Sure, at first glance, your friends are merely "supporting" their buddy and helping him get his life back together. But have they heard you out and respected your feelings about what this guy did to you? Did they understand his offense in the first place? No. They don't "get" sexual assault, or they wouldn't refer to "the person you think hurt you," as if you imagined the relentless grabbing and the fleeing and all of it.

They don't understand the difference between making a blind-drunk pass at someone and deliberately grabbing and chasing and laughing all the while. They don't know what it feels like to see that kind of malice in someone's eyes. That's why this jerk haunts your dreams and makes you anxious when you see him. His intention—to make you feel small and powerless—was crystal clear to you. What he wanted you to know, at some cellular level, even in his boozy state, was that even after years of friendship and trust between you you're still just a piece of ass to him.

When someone gets drunk and uses racial epithets at a friend out of the blue, what does that say? It says, "Some part of me wants to cut you down to size." That's racist culture and it's asshole culture and it's also just being an unmitigated asshole to the core. Your ex-friend has demonstrated a similar kind of hatred.

Your reaction to this guy is natural and justified. Your anxiety makes perfect sense. You don't want to be around him. You tried not to make things worse for his wife, but you told your friends. You wanted to protect them and yourself.

Your two friends may think they're helping him and that you're heartless for staying focused on something he did when he was drunk. But that's misguided. He never apologized. He never came clean. He never confronted the beast he became when he drank. That beast is still there. If he'd handled things differently, acknowledged that he did terrible things, that would be different. You still wouldn't want anything to do with him, but you would at least know that he'd faced his actions. Instead, your mutual friends have helped him take a shortcut. That was shortsighted of them, and it sprang from their essential misunderstanding of his offenses. They didn't call you to talk about the fact that they were supporting him or consider how it might affect you. They didn't ask you questions about what you went through. They took the easy way out.

You SENSED this all along. You chose to assume they understood your pain but they wanted to support their friend. You addressed the situation with the two of them directly, you agreed to disagree, and you moved on. Perfectly mature and not a bad choice. But do you see how YOU had to do the bending and they didn't do a thing to facilitate that? Then you saw the friend interacting with the jerk, and it upset you. Totally natural that it would upset you. You confronted him.

And while it probably wasn't completely fair to take him to task for being friends with this guy when you'd said you accepted it, what came out of that interaction? *You learned that he never took your account seriously.* His attitude was "Fuck what you *think* happened; you're wrong. I wasn't there, but I've decided independently that you're making it up." That was under the surface of your interactions with that friend all along.

Fuck that guy. He's not your friend.

Sure, it wasn't all that prudent of you to start hurling angry words at him over Facebook. But does that make YOU the culprit here? No, it does not. You were angry because the creepy predator ex-friend's attack on you is a haunting thing in your life. Why is it a haunting thing? Because he grabbed your body violently, in public, and laughed in your face while he was doing it. "See how small you feel? See how little you mean to me?" He's attracted to you and can't stand the power you wield over him, so he has to make you feel demeaned and pathetic. That dynamic is as old as time, and it's one of the most frightening things a woman can face.

Some people believe that every aggressive sexual act or unwelcome advance adds up to the same thing. My personal feeling is that context and attitude matter a great fucking deal, both in how we define an act and in how quickly we might be expected to "recover" from it. In your case, your ex-friend's actions and his attitude sent a very strong message: "You're not a person to me. You don't exist. Years of friendship, professional affiliation, mutual friends: It all adds up to nothing. You are nothing to me. Your feelings don't matter; your thoughts don't matter. You're still JUST A WOMAN. When you say, 'Stop!' I'll laugh at you, because your words add up to nothing."

You had power over him, so he wanted to erase you. Acts of malice stay with the body. They are not easily forgotten.

Because what you're describing is not a bit of drunken, idiotic grabbiness or unfortunate cluelessness. It's malignant and purposefully demeaning. I suspect that most women reading this know exactly what that energy feels like. We've been there. It's different.

It takes some explaining for guys like your two friends to get it, having never been close to that particular kind of malice. Maybe it would make you feel better to describe it to them in writing so they'll get it. Maybe they need to have the cruelty of that act explained to them. Maybe they need to hear that until this guy apologizes directly to you, you aren't about to take his "reformation" seriously. It should've happened a long time ago. If he wanted to live in your community, he should've addressed what he did to you and anyone else he hurt or disrespected.

Otherwise, what the fuck? It's amazing, the horseshit we expect women to swallow and act like it's honey.

And now *you're* the bad guy because you exploded? And even *you* believe that! Your mistake was that you tried to push your emotions aside and accept a situation that is un-fucking-acceptable. Trust me, I'm all for pushing emotions aside and dealing when life requires it. But you can't forgive and forget, because it turns out you're still angry.

Why? Because they aren't listening to you. They think you're needlessly stirring up trouble. I would write to them and explain to them what malice feels like. I would explain that their friend hurt many people, and that hurt is real, and those people don't want to see his fucking face anymore for a very good reason.

Then I'd move on, knowing you've expressed yourself clearly, not through a chat on Facebook, but on paper.

Is that the wisest thing to do? I can't say for sure. The wisest thing might be just to accept that these guys are blind and stay out of their lives. They have the luxury of not having to see. And they have the luxury of not having to see the *luxury* of their blindness. They would rather call the seeing world crazy than open their fucking eyes. But if you feel strongly enough about it, you may owe it to yourself to address your feelings with them, if only for your own peace of mind.

It's okay. Your eyes are wide open.

Polly

Commitmentphobes of N.Y.C.

Dear Polly,

What is the deal with all these thirtysomething men who say they "aren't looking for a relationship at all right now"? I see it as a product of New York City being a grown-ups' playground where men are enabled to act like children until they are fifty or sixty (or older?!) or maybe they are deeply wounded from their last relationship or maybe they have just gotten too good at being alone and just having another body in their bed makes it impossible for them to sleep. This state of mind doesn't make sense to me, because I thought the point of life is to make connections with other people and opting out of relationships makes you inhuman. Like "No thanks, I don't breathe oxygen."

I don't feel this way, so I know this isn't my problem. Except I feel like I keep on meeting these men with whom there's a mutual attraction, affection, and easy rapport in conversation, only to find out that they have the intimacy chip missing. I know I can't do anything to change a person who says things like "I'm not looking for a relationship." So what do I do? And what is their deal? And how does this madness stop?!

Love,
I'm Great So Why Don't You Love Me?

—ɯ—

Dear IGSWDYLM,

When I was thirty-four years old, I went on a date with a very attractive, extremely smart guy. We'd e-mailed back and forth a lot before that, so it was pretty much on no matter what. But just as things were getting interesting, he said, "Of course, I'm not looking to get serious at this point." I smiled and said, "That's okay, I'm trying to avoid jumping into anything too fast, too. If everything goes really well, you could maybe be Boyfriend #5." He laughed and I excused myself to go to the bathroom, where I closed my eyes and thought, "GODDAMN IT, NOT THIS AGAIN. I CAN'T FUCKING DO THIS AGAIN." My last relationship had ended when my boyfriend couldn't commit to marriage. The boyfriend before that talked about commitment all the time, but whenever we discussed the future, he always sounded wishy-washy, if not downright skeptical. "NOTHING WILL EVER WORK OUT. I'M DOOMED. I'LL SPEND THE REST OF MY LIFE BEGGING GUYS TO BE WITH ME."

Eventually, I talked myself down. "It's okay," I told myself. "This is a first date. Don't say a word about this. He likes you. Don't ask questions about how he feels. Don't dig. Just smile along, have fun, and then say good night."

I returned to the table. We chatted and had a good time. I didn't push it. I said good night. We went out again a week later. I did not fire questions at him. I did not sleep with him. You could say that I was faking it, playing by *The Rules,* but actually I was protecting myself. I didn't want to get emotionally invested and then figure out that it wasn't going anywhere. I didn't want to demean myself by playing the desperate thirty-four-year-old woman with the biological clock ticking down. I'd had my share of spontaneous fun with guys for years. This time, I was going to keep myself safe from harm. I was going to resist acting like an insecure wreck—which, by the way, I was capable of doing even with men I didn't like that much. I'd done it many times before, with all kinds of unworthy dudes. It was just a compulsion, really. I always had to say the one thing I wasn't supposed to say.

My plan was to get to know a handful of guys and put off going out with anyone seriously for as long as possible. Why take some guy seriously just because we started sleeping together? Fuck that. Even if Boyfriend #1 lived across the country and Boyfriends #2 and 3 were really just friends so far and Boyfriend #4 flirted with the waitress a little too much on our first date, I needed to keep thinking of myself as a scientist, collecting data from a remove, making smart, logical choices.

It felt good to embrace logic, even if my lizard brain sometimes screamed, "NOT ANOTHER FLINCHY DUDE! I CAN'T TAKE IT!" in the privacy of a bathroom stall.

Three weeks later, my date told me he was dumping all his girlfriends. I said, "Poor ladies." A few days after that, he asked about my boyfriends—specifically, if I could break up with them. I said sure. He seemed worth it.

A year and a half later, we got married. I know, gross. Same old smug fairy tale. Same old "Look at me, I played my cards just right and tricked a guy into marriage." But that's not what I'm trying to tell you with my story. I'm trying to show you that just as most women insist that they're looking for something serious, most guys (yes, particularly in New York) say they *aren't* looking for anything serious. These are just the sounds we make. You can't get twisted in a knot over it at first. You have to roll with it.

So this is what I'd advise: three or four dates of rolling with it—not to lure a hapless motherfucker into some elaborate trap, but to protect yourself from feeling like a beggar.

Because you aren't a beggar! You should never feel that way! Even if you feel a little disingenuous saying, "I'm trying to avoid getting too invested over the wrong person," when you feel like you're already in love with the person in front of you, that's okay. You *should* be more cautious about falling in love too quickly, shouldn't you? You *shouldn't* invest in the wrong guy prematurely. What if he's kind of a dick on the third date? What if, when you do sleep together, the sex isn't great and it doesn't improve over time? And you're already semi-committed? What if it turns out he's anxious, depressed, broke, allergic to kids, and about to move to another country?

For the record, in the good old days, I totally slept with anxious, depressed, broke, kid-allergic guys without thinking about it for a second. That was my target demographic, even. But let's be practical. When you're in your thirties and you know you want to have kids, should you risk getting involved with that guy, then waste a decade struggling to make him cheer up and grow up and love kids and deal? Why not marry a plastic garden gnome instead? It would be a lot less taxing and stressful.

When you know what you want, you have to keep your heart and your eyes wide open. You have to be willing to fall in love, but you also have to be willing to step back and say, "No way, this is not a good choice for me," before it's too late. If you're walking around lamenting all the noncommittal guys, that's going to distract you from the fact that you still get to choose. It's completely natural to think, "Oh my Christ, these guys with their loner bullshit!" It's like noticing that the sky is blue. But don't let that make you forget your value. Don't feel like you're asking permission from someone else just to get a tiny bit of consideration and attention.

This is why having firm boundaries from the start is important. You have to remember that you're gathering information at first. It will still make your heart sink when you hear that he's not ready for anything serious, but you have to stay cool and ride it out. Even if he acts like he's ready to get married tonight, wait and see—if he's on drugs or just wants to get into your pants or what. You must stay open and observe. You must control yourself. You must not treat men like they'll fix all of your problems. You must not treat yourself like you *need* someone to fix all of your problems. That's not fair to *you*.

What do you want from your life? Who do you want to be in ten years? What are your strengths and your flaws? You have to know the answers to these questions. When you do, you will be able to say to your date, "I am a regular, flawed person. I'm not here to close the deal at all costs. If there's something that feels wrong, that's okay. That tells us we're not a match." Easy come, easy go. Letting the wrong ones show their true stripes is just as important as letting the right ones show their true strengths.

Does that sound too clinical? Well, you know what's worse than feeling too clinical about dating? Feeling like a beggar all the time. *That* feeling is what you *really* hate the most. You don't hate the flinchy guys. Why do they matter? You just hate that feeling of asking a flinchy guy for a favor. "I know you're not into relationships, but will you date me anyway? I know you really only want sex from me, but will you love me anyway?" Instead, you can say, "You sound indifferent about this. Maybe we're not a match. I don't want to get serious too fast, but I also don't want to tool around with just anyone. I believe in true love." See how it works? You can say what you believe in without writing a lukewarm dude into your story.

The bottom line is: It doesn't matter if New York City is filled with noncommittal motherfuckers. You don't need to change the population of New York City. You can keep bumping into these kinds of guys over and over, and it means nothing. It doesn't alter your future. You just have to know yourself and know that you won't settle for something half-assed. You can be alone for as long as it takes. Can't you? Isn't it good to be alive? If it's not, fix *that*. But in the meantime, borrow a little of that single-guy apathy, and make a rational assessment of what you see. Slow down and tolerate the meaningless patter. Hold your own space and honor yourself and don't let that space shrink or collapse in the company of indifference. Don't ask indifference to love you. Indifference can go fuck itself. This is your life, and it's going to be big and bright and beautiful.

Polly

III

Reckoning, Anger, and Obsession

The Cheat Sheet

Polly,

I'm a new reader and dig your crazy no-bullshit advice. But I'm writing not so much for advice but to throw down the gauntlet. My understanding is that always ends well.

The subject is me cheating on my wife. I'm sick of feeling guilty about wanting to, and rationally I'm having a hard time figuring out why I shouldn't because I think it may actually help our marriage and improve the chances of us providing a happy home for our children. Clearly a convenient conclusion, but one I've done a lot of thinking about.

Here are the supporting facts:

1. My wife is no longer interested in sex. She is too busy and tired from stressing over the kids and delivering our little royals to their next playdate to generate biological feelings for me. Before the children were born, we had a "zestful" sexual relationship, but no longer.
2. It is said men in general have a much higher sex drive. I am a man and find this to be a considerably large understatement, along the lines of saying *Transformers* might be a shitty movie.
3. I find my wife sexy; I also find other women sexy. Some of these women will have sex with me, and we will enjoy it.

4. Having sex with other women will relieve much of the emotional resentment I have against my wife for her sexual indifference (even though I empathize with her), and we will have a better emotional relationship as a lack of sex will no longer be a source of conflict.

5. I will feel physically better if I have sex with other women because I will be released from the buzzing, thrumming miasma of lust that plagues me every moment during a sexless week. Believe me, most men are familiar with these feelings.

6. My wife is an outstanding mother and otherwise a good wife and best friend.

7. I believe my children will be happier raised in a home with a caring mother and father present.

8. My wife and I have spoken about my inescapable need for physical affection; we have tried methods to rekindle her physical passions, but to no avail.

9. Deep down, I believe she would tolerate my affairs as long as I was safe, respectful, and discreet and continued to be a good father and husband. I think she would prefer that approach over a frank discussion about open marriage, which would hurt and offend her with its brazenness. I would rather carry the burden of culpability than dispel her sense of our family.

10. Affairs with other women will not change my love for her.

Finally—and this is more of an observation—if gay men can maintain their marriages while entertaining outside engagements, isn't it biased and unrealistic to punish their heterosexual peers for addressing the same urges?

My challenge to you is to make a compelling case why, on balance, I should not pursue outside affairs in the interests of my family's longevity and happiness, provided the facts above. I don't think you can.

Sincerely,
Cheating Gauntlet Man

—⟋ⴲ⟍—

Dear CGM,

Cheating is called cheating for a reason. The issue on the table is honesty, not sex. If the lack of sex in your relationship poses a serious threat to your marriage, you should sit down with your wife and tell her that. You should ask to see a couples therapist together. You should say that you need her to commit to some concrete plan for changing things between you, whether that means letting someone watch the kids one afternoon and one evening per week so you can have time together, or deciding on a minimum fooling-around schedule, or reading a book about sex therapy and then talking about it, or some combination of those things. Tell her that you need to know that things are going to change, because your frustration and powerlessness in this area are affecting your outlook on your life and your marriage.

Here's what you shouldn't do: assume that your wife would be fine with you discreetly running around town, fucking other women, or that she'd prefer that scenario to discussing this openly. Because I can personally fucking guarantee you, your wife would rather talk about it. She is not remotely okay with you fucking around. You've been watching too much *Mad Men*. Making a rousing argument for fucking other women on the sneak is a pretty elaborate way to justify something that's unjustifiable. It's a brave-looking way of being a total chickenshit.

Fucking other people when your wife thinks that you two

are monogamous is dishonest, hurtful, and beyond insulting. It's the kind of thing that many people never, ever get over. It's the kind of thing that will lead to you, alone, in a one-bedroom apartment, while your sexy, wonderful wife remarries someone handsome and loyal and honest who makes his desires known instead of hiding behind logic and lists.

Married gay people who screw around on the side tend to have conversations about it first. The difference between discussing it openly and honestly and just sneaking around behind someone's back is enormous. Having an open marriage and cheating are two entirely different things. The former is a choice. The latter is a crime that's willfully committed against the other person. When you cheat on someone, you betray their trust, you rip apart their love for you, you embarrass the hell out of them, you depress them (in this case, at a time when she has little people who depend on her and she can't really afford to be depressed beyond belief), and you permanently alter their ability to respect you. Do you know how bad that feels, loving and believing in someone more than anyone else and then having your love injured irreparably?

It's unspeakably arrogant to assume that your wife will never find out so you don't have to examine any of these very real consequences. How often do you think random women who sleep with married men end up telling the wives about the affairs? How often do you think wives find out by other means? All the fucking time.

To me, what really works about marriage is the feeling that you have someone on your side, who would never do anything to hurt you. When that person betrays you, it's hard to get that feeling back. And in the company of children, believing in your partner is unquestionably crucial—it's intoxicating, really. You know that you're supported and cared for. Having that support and trust and care ripped from you, when there are little kids in the picture, could make someone feel more vulnerable and heartsick than you can possibly imagine.

I know you think I'm being dramatic. I am not being dramatic.

Now, to be fair, I think that for heterosexual men, what really works about marriage is the feeling that you have a woman on your side, who loves you and loves your kids and who is also very attracted to you. When that person rejects you, over and over again, it's hard to get that feeling of well-being back. Believing in your marriage and having regular sex with your wife is also unquestionably crucial, and intoxicating, really. Having that support and attention ripped from you, when there are little kids in the picture, could make a man feel more vulnerable and heartsick than his wife can possibly imagine.

If that feels accurate to you, then my guess is that you don't really want to sleep with random women as much as you think you do. What you really want is to feel desired and adored by your wife, whom you love very much. You feel invisible. You feel like she doesn't want or even love you anymore.

Your challenge in this situation is to show up and make yourself vulnerable, not to disappear and force her into an inherently vulnerable position. Your challenge is to resist the urge to avenge your wife's lack of desire (by fucking other women). Even though you've gone to elaborate lengths to make this form of punishment appear harmless and logical, on some level this is about you feeling hurt and neglected and powerless to change it.

When you feel hurt and vulnerable and you're willing to talk openly about it? That's an opportunity for your marriage to grow into something more beautiful than it was before. You already have a decent marriage. Don't run away and protect yourself and lie and hide and fuck yourself and your kids over in the process. That may be the easy way out in the short term. In the long term, though, you'll drop a bomb in the middle of your life, and you won't be able to pick up the pieces once it goes off.

Honesty. That's all you need. You need to go to your wife and be very honest about your sexual needs. If she waves you off and doesn't listen, don't accept that. Make her understand that this is a gigantic thing in your life, and your marriage is at stake.

Now, I have to admit, I'm sort of wondering how involved you are with your little royals. You talk about your wife ushering them hither and thither, but not you. And you seem to assume that you'll have plenty of free time to wander off and fuck other women. Does your wife have that kind of free time? If she wanted to have an affair, could she conceivably free up her schedule to fuck someone on the sly? I'm guessing that she's running around in circles, picking little shoes up off the floor, or waking up in the middle of the night with a sick kid, or doing another load of laundry because you forgot. While you imagine fucking other women, what is your wife doing? Loading the dishwasher? Sleeping, because she never gets enough sleep and she feels exhausted all the time because she never has a second to herself?

If so, I would suggest that you get to know your little royals a little better. Tell your wife that you're going to take Saturdays from ten to four, and she can do whatever she wants. Her interest in sucking your cock may experience an uptick under such circumstances.

But if your kids are very little and your wife is very, very busy with them in ways that you could be, too, if you got off your smug ass and made it so, yet you sit back and watch her rushing around in circles and you still expect her to keep everything running AND fuck you every night once the kids are tucked away? You really should divorce your wife and hire a housekeeper, a nanny, and a live-in sex worker instead. Because that's the level of service you seem to require.

I suggest you spend more time with your kids, and also more time thinking about what's best for them, so the burden of stress doesn't always rest on your wife. Find out how you can do more around the house so your wife is less annoyed with you. Meditate. Exercise more often to burn off all of that free-floating lust. But more than anything else, learn to speak honestly to your wife. Explain to her what your minimum needs are, and (IMPORTANT!) ask her what her minimum needs are in order to feel happy. Explain that you really feel like your marriage will suffer horribly if you don't have more sex, and (IMPORTANT!) ask her if you can't watch the kids more or take over the dishes every night so she can read a book. Say, "I'll put the kids down, then we make out right after that, then I'll do all the dishes while you go to sleep." Believe me that there are ways to entice her.

Obviously, you need to adjust your expectations a little about how much sex you can have, and she needs to adjust her expectations that sex can only happen when she's totally in the mood. Sometimes you get in the mood by going for it, plain and simple. Sometimes you get in the mood by saying, "Well, it's Friday at 3:00 p.m. and we're home alone. It's now or never." Sometimes you get in the mood by watching your husband usher the royals to a playdate while you flip through a magazine for once in your sorry life.

I know, it's all so romantic. The faster you accept that having a family sometimes means not fucking like rabbits whenever the mood strikes, the faster you're going to wake up to a new paradigm that isn't as compromised and flat as it sounds; it's just different. The sex is actually just as good. We were built for it. Everyone gets worked up over how it should start, how it should unfold, how spontaneous it should be, how much it should resemble a scene out of *Top Gun,* all blowing curtains and plinky soft rock. Sex itself is pretty excellent with or without the candles and the plinky plonk.

Now, I would address the idea of an open marriage, but I think you need to completely redesign your marriage to accommodate your wife's and your needs before you think about that option. And anyway, open marriage means both of you can have sex with other people. It doesn't mean that you can but she can't. (I've heard of this arrangement, and sorry, but it's sexist and idiotic.) That path is pretty perilous, particularly with kids in the picture. Maybe they can swing it in France. If I had access to lots of red wine and stinky cheese and smoking-hot Parisian men, I might pry open my sad little heteronormative mind to just about anything.

But you haven't really worked on your sex life in earnest yet. It's understandable that this is not your wife's top priority, but if you're really contemplating cheating as much as you seem to be, then you'll be doing her a big favor by making the bleakness of your current outlook very, very clear to her. She needs to stop waiting for magic to happen and start making a concrete effort to meet you halfway. You need to meet her halfway, too. If I were the one charged with handling the lion's share of the kid-related shit, I don't think I could look my husband in the eye without sneering, let alone fuck him.

Right now, you are keeping a big part of who you are hidden. As long as you're lying, you can't have a good marriage. More lying won't fix that.

Polly

I'm Tired of Being So Nice

Dear Polly,

I am trying to figure out how to be less nice. I don't want to be less generous or less kind, just less nice. You know what I mean—that craven, smiley, oh-gosh-no-of-course-go-ahead-of-me, laughing-at-every-unfunny-joke, acting-thrilled-to-see-people-who-treat-me-like-shit veneer. It degrades my life. It has always degraded my life. I am only now starting to understand how much. I'm mad about it.

I've always been "nice." Obviously, that doesn't make me a particularly good person. I've done plenty of vile shit. The older I get, the more I have to pry my desperate grasp off the idea that niceness somehow gives me value (it is THE thing that gives me value). That it obligates the world to treat me well in return. I mean, I have long known that this does not work, and yet I kept/keep doing it. Mostly what being nice buys me is a load of bullshit from most people, a lack of respect from the people I admire, and a frightening well of anger that is fed when things don't go in accordance with my stupid broken theory that I don't believe in anyway.

Here is what I mean by nice: I am so good at feigning fascination that deeply unfascinating people waylay me at every opportunity to get some more of the ego food I'm always dishing out. It means that I attract people who can't tolerate a single unflattering remark about themselves and who will turn vicious the second I let my genial admiration go slack. It means that when people try to take things from me, my automatic response is to give those things, and that it costs me a ton in guilt/shame/fear not to give in to people immediately. I assess my value in how much people "like" me, even when I don't like them, and even when I see their contempt for me growing every time I don't stand up for myself. Even when I dislike them. Even when I truly hate them.

It means I have always had narcissists in my life. It means that when I try to talk to my new boyfriend (who very clearly wants the best for me) about some minor adjustments I need to make to our relationship, I think, "It would be easier to just break up." It means I let my ex-boyfriend and an ex-boss simultaneously almost destroy me, because who could be mean to someone so nice? I must be getting what I deserve. It means that when I say a necessary no, I have a moment of triumph and then spend the rest of the day under an avalanche of guilt. It means I try to redirect the conversation when anyone makes a bigoted remark instead of saying, "Um, EXCUSE ME?" It means I want to sink into the floor when someone rightly says to me, "Um, EXCUSE ME?"

What I want is to be *actually* kind. I want to give things where they're needed. Or even wanted! But I want to do it consciously, not by reflex, not because the cost of saying no is so absurdly high I can't deal with it. I want to be able to say, "You hurt me," when I'm hurt. I want to be able to say, "I don't like that." I want to be able to say, "I'm leaving now," instead of sitting in a meeting for two hours past the time I said I absolutely had to leave.

Polly, what do I DO with this? What do I do with all this fakery and anger and saccharine sweetness? What if I do dispose of my niceness and what's left is something no one likes? Help me, help me please!

Pleadingly,
Nicely Nicely

—ɯ—

Dear NN,

The strange irony of being a very sensitive person who wants to say, "I don't like that," or "You hurt me," is that *you* tend to take it too personally when *other* people say, "I don't like that," or "You hurt me." You feel attacked, and so you conclude that the other person must be "wrong" to say something so direct, so critical, so negative. So you avoid asserting yourself the same way that other people do, because other people will surely encounter your assertiveness as injurious, the way you have.

Here's the thing: Being nice is worthless if you're just going to feel resentful about it in the end. You might as well just be outspoken and state your needs from the outset. Because as much as people resent assertive women, they resent disingenuous, overly friendly, secretly furious women even more.

Maybe you need to ask yourself, "How secretly furious am I?"

I can certainly understand why you'd feel so angry. By simply showing up and being a woman, you're asked to satisfy an incredibly tangled and contradictory set of demands. You are supposed to be assertive but not *too* assertive. You are supposed to speak your mind but only on subjects about which everyone already agrees. You are supposed to toe the party line while pretending that it's your personal choice.

Trust me, I've been there. So this is what I want you to accept, first and foremost: You are a nice person, and you're also full of anger. You're a walking tangle of contradictions. That's okay. Most of us are like that. Women, most of all. How could we not be? People want us to be sexy warriors who roll over and play dead on command. They want us to be flirty burlesque dancers in burkas, aggressive conquistadors with cookies in the oven, Dorothy Parker meets Dorothy Gale, Sandra

Bernhard meets Sandra Dee, Kristen Stewart meets Martha Stewart.

Experiments in asking for exactly what you want will go badly. Do it anyway. Do it and expect people to react badly. Because you're sensitive, you won't like this. Think about how they feel, and try to empathize. Think about how you might soften your message. Watch how other people do it. I know it sounds like a management technique, but good communicators usually start with something positive, then move to the negative gently: "I love this about you, but I have to draw the line here." "I know you're trying your best, but this is what I still need from you." "I care about you so much and you're such an important friend to me, but I don't think I can do this one thing."

Listen closely when someone asserts his or her boundaries. Because that's healthy behavior, even if it's not to your taste at this point. Learn from them. Because most people avoid problems instead of asserting themselves. They clam up. They disappear. That's the coward's path, even if it's a path a lot of us take.

I used to admire people who could hang with anything. Now the women I admire the most are women who never pretend to be different than they are. Women like that express their anger. They admit when they're down. They don't beat themselves up over their bad moods. They allow themselves to be grumpy sometimes. They grant themselves the right to be grouchy, or to say nothing, or to decline your offer without a lengthy explanation.

Sometimes it seems like the rest of us are on a never-ending self-improvement conveyor belt. We're running faster and faster, struggling to be our best selves, but every day we fail and we hate ourselves for it.

Fuck that. Let's be mortal. Let's not be sexy warrior princesses or burlesque dancers in burkas or conquistadors with cookies in the oven. How many years do we have to wait just to speak our minds? Let's be flinty and unreasonable instead. Let's tell the truth, *without* a smile. Let's let our words drop, one by one, without explanation, without apology, like the first few pebbles before a landslide.

Polly

The Weight of Rage

Hi, Polly,

I have always been a "big" girl. Growing up, I was always in the ninety to ninety-fifth percentile of height and weight. I grew up with a mother who admonished me to eat less and suck in my stomach. I've been sucking in my stomach and worrying about my figure since I was six. I was on an experimental weight-loss drug in middle school. I was in Weight Watchers when I was thirteen. All in my mom's efforts to get me to lose weight. But I'm a grown lady now, and I'm sick to death of my family's comments and concerns about my weight, my food, and my health. It hurts my feelings and makes me feel like a child, and I'm about to come unglued on the people I love most.

Growing up with that kind of scrutiny and pressure has irreparably poisoned my relationship with my mother. I don't like her to touch me, and any comment she makes about me feels like a damning judgment. I didn't even take her with me when I shopped for my wedding gown, because I wanted to feel confident and pretty when I made such a big decision. These things you're supposed to do with your mother I did alone rather than subject myself to what she might possibly say. Even my dad will sometimes do things that hurt my feelings, like express shock that I went to the gym.

My husband is suffering from the anger I feel whenever my weight or health is brought up; I automatically jump to the conclusion that anything he wants to do that's health-related is actually because I'm fat. He only has good intentions for us to be healthy and to bond together.

I'm able to shop wherever I feel like shopping. I am perfectly healthy, with normal cholesterol and normal blood pressure, according to my doctor visit last week. I'm a nice-looking person. I look good in my clothes. I was a beautiful bride. I just really like food. I feel like I need some kind of framed document asserting that I am healthy, that I am FINE, but even then I don't think I'd be left alone about it. Now I'm newly married to a man who wants me to eat well and live well, and every time I talk about food and he looks at me, I project onto him disapproval, revulsion, disgust. I feel myself doing this. I want it to stop, lest it poison my marriage.

Why won't my parents leave me alone? Even my mother acknowledges she could have ignored my baby fat and I probably would have lost it naturally as a teen. I know they mean well and they're hounding me because they love me or whatever, but they're hurting my feelings to a degree I don't think they understand; I'm sitting here crying and writing to an advice columnist, after all. I'm so angry and so hurt. Why can't I get the acceptance from them that I want so desperately, that it has taken YEARS of therapy and self-care for me to give myself? My happiness would improve exponentially if they would just realize this topic is off-limits. What can I do? How can I set this boundary and have it stick? What would you do if you were me?

Sincerely,
Just a Normal Girl

—⟶⟵—

Dear JANG,

If I were you, I would forward this letter to your mother. She might not understand at first. It might make her angry.

She might say, "How dare you call me out for the ONE thing I did wrong, when all I wanted was for you to be healthy and happy?" She might write you off as crazy, in spite of the fact that your letter couldn't be clearer or more heartbreaking.

But I would forward your letter to her anyway. I would do it because you are haunted by her bad decisions, every day of your life, and you need to spell that out. Because it's starting to affect your ability to love her—and yourself, and everybody else. You're so angry that you can't see her clearly anymore, and I don't think that will improve unless you tell her. It sounds like she's reasonably rational and not insanely defensive about this, so directly addressing it doesn't threaten to further damage your relationship. You need to be gentle; get your husband or a friend to edit out anything that might be perceived as an attack. But it's time to declare talk about your weight, exercise, and eating OFF-LIMITS. You want to love her and enjoy her company. You need this. You need to know she won't push you into that space anymore. You want to be free from that awful space. And who wouldn't?

Even knowing what we all know about eating disorders today, many parents don't understand how fundamentally unkind it is to disrupt a kid's natural relationship to food. When you tell a fucking six-year-old that she needs to watch her figure, you're interrupting her natural development, her understanding of what food is, how it feels to be full, and how it feels to be hungry. You're training her to see a fat person in the mirror.

I'm not some health guru. I like cheese and bread and bread and cheese, to infinity and beyond. But when I was a teenager, I watched my friend's mother hover around her, commenting on her weight every time she had a snack. She even posted a photo of her daughter in a bikini on the fridge so she'd be reminded of her own body *every time she ate*. I watched as she got smaller and smaller, eating an apple and a Diet Coke for lunch every day. She didn't look healthy anymore. She didn't seem happy anymore. And her entire experience—of herself, of food—was forever changed. Her relationship to her body and to food wouldn't be easy or natural or relaxed for a long time after that. She would have to work hard for fifteen years to fix those mistakes.

This is one of those well-intentioned things that parents get dramatically wrong, over and over again. It doesn't take overt body shaming, either. All it takes is being a parent who sees a kid's decisions as a natural extension of his or her own. "I would stop eating right now, so you should, too. I would try my damnedest to be skinnier, so you'd better try your damnedest, too." It's like trying to turn your children into an extension of yourself, instead of welcoming the fact that they are completely different and separate and independent.

As a parent, you *do* have to constantly remind yourself that you are not a god, molding a human in your own image. You are merely supporting whatever your child chooses to become, even if those choices don't always thrill you. It's easy enough to embrace and support a toddler who loves dolphins or playing house. It's harder to accept and appreciate a fully grown human who has her own body and her own ideas.

So, look, the reasons for your anger and frustration couldn't be more clear, and they're completely justified. I think you need to express them. I don't think you'll be happy until you do.

It's a complicated problem, but it has a simple solution: Draw boundaries and stick to them. Express the emotional side of it with care; go into detail if you want. But then shift gears and tell your family precisely what you expect from them: "No more talk about weight, food, or how I look. None." Don't apologize for it. Don't second-guess yourself. Don't get mad if you can help it. Just say, "Hey, this is what I need."

I have a friend who knows how to confidently ask for what he wants from people. It's amazing how effective it is and how successful and charismatic you can be if you stay calm and ask people what you want from them without seeming to take offense. He presupposes that people will *want* to help him, and then they do. He sets boundaries, too, without making it personal. "I don't do that." "I would never agree to a plan like that." "This is how I like to do it." As women, we often want to bend and adjust and please other people first, and then we find ourselves resenting it. Don't let that happen to you, JANG.

Things will improve. If your parents mess up—and they will—don't overreact. Turn and look at them silently, as if to say, "We've talked about this, remember?" Making a giant stink about it every time it comes up will only make you more upset. You can calmly restate your boundaries. That will bring better results in the long run than getting angry and going off.

So that's the practical advice I have for you. On the emotional side, I understand why you'd be really angry and why you'd project that anger onto your husband. You're assuming that he feels the same way about your weight as your family does. You have to work hard to deconstruct this belief. I would explain to your husband that you need to do some therapeutic exercises around this, where you relax and talk and he reminds you that he thinks you're beautiful and he's attracted to you and loves you the way you are. Most marriages need something like this built into the woodwork, a time when both partners can hear the things they need to hear repeatedly. For many of us, it can be challenging to pinpoint exactly what will make us feel better. It takes work. And maybe what you need from your husband isn't about how you look at all; maybe it's about him loving you no matter what. Lots of people want that. "I will love you even if all your hair falls out. I will love you even if both your arms fall off." It's kind of comical, but it also goes to the heart of what you went through as a kid. "You're not good until you get smaller. You won't be okay with us until you're the right shape." *Fuck being the right shape. I'm your kid! Love me as I am!*

I know it hurts. I can relate to that feeling. There was a time when I could barely stand to visit my mother. I was going through a sad and angry period, and I just wanted to say, *"Look at me! This is who I am! I'm complicated! I'm not a happy clown! You have to love me anyway!"* But sometimes my mother is afraid of complicated. Eventually, I figured it out; she always assumed my anger and frustration were about her, that I was angry *at her,* and not just lonely or depressed. Sure, I wrote her letters. I ranted and I raged. But that only confirmed her suspicion that I was unstable. What worked was saying, "I am in a shitty mood this morning. It's not about you, so don't think that it is, okay? I love you. Just be patient with me." And once I could say that to her, and she could hear me, it changed everything.

I bet you're a lot wiser and a lot stronger than your parents in many ways. They may have felt much less loved than you felt growing up, even if your upbringing was compromised in some ways. You have to express your anger, too. But when you do, do it from a loving place. Do it knowing that it will make everyone feel more clear about what is and isn't appropriate.

Having healthy, clear boundaries can actually bring people closer to each other. By telling people exactly what you expect, what you will and won't do, what you want and what you don't want from them, you will put them at ease. Only crazy motherfuckers encounter healthy boundaries as an insult. I don't think your parents are crazy motherfuckers. They messed up in the past, but they're not malicious; they're just clueless. I bet they feel pretty guilty, too. I bet they feel sad about how things turned out between you.

Once you demand a compassionate space where you can feel safe from judgment, you'll feel more compassionate toward them. Once you forgive yourself for standing up for what you want, and not becoming what *they* defined as perfect, you'll have room to forgive them. If you work hard and expect setbacks and stay firm in your beliefs, you'll get there. I know you're angry and hurt. It'll take a long time. But you'll get there.

It will never be perfect, of course. That's okay. Imperfect things are even better. You know that better than anyone. Imperfect things are the most beautiful things of all.

Polly

Cheaters Become You

Dear Polly,

I'm in my mid-twenties, and I've developed a pattern of getting involved with attached men. At first, I thought (pretended?) it was a coincidence, but at this point it's clear that I am the common denominator.

There was the guy who DID break up with his girlfriend as promised, but then I said (honestly) that I couldn't trust him and wouldn't date him—but proceeded to hook up with him again months later, after he had started a new relationship. There were a few inappropriate one-off-ish hookups with guys who were unavailable, a couple of walking-a-thin-line ongoing text things with married co-workers at a former job (yes, using the *m*-word horrifies me), and most recently an awful, drawn-out situation with a co-worker at my new job. We'll call him Aaron.

The Aaron situation has felt by far the worst. It started with an instantaneous attraction/friendship/spark, even though he's not at all my usual type physically. The night we met at a house party, we spent the entire time talking one-on-one in a kitchen alcove, and I got immediate friend requests/follows from him, only to find out from mutual friends that not only did he have a serious long-term girlfriend but she had been there that night, being ignored while he blatantly flirted with me. Aaron and I connected at a few happy hours in the following month, two of which resulted in car make-out sessions (like high school all over again). After that, I had a flash of morality or fear and told him not to pursue me any further. Nothing happened for a few months, save some excessive eye contact.

In May, a close male friend who's also a co-worker sat me down and told me I was damaging my personal and professional reputation by being involved with Aaron. Obviously, this resulted in tears, mortification, and above all shame. Particularly because I felt I had ultimately done the right thing and had essentially chosen to NOT get involved with him. My friend didn't believe that I never slept with him; apparently, rumors were swirling heavily. Our relationship was strained for months, he and I not speaking, which was just awful. Then the friendship recovered. Aaron broke up with his girlfriend and immediately dated yet another co-worker of ours. I believe now that he didn't cut ties with the first girlfriend, just kept two relationships going at once (in different cities). Obviously, a pretty terrible guy.

About a month ago, I saw Aaron, and we spent the entire night talking one-on-one again. A few nights later, we ended up leaving a bar together (where many co-workers were present; he seems to lack remorse and/or any kind of discretion; maybe he just knows that he always gets away with things) but not sleeping together. Two weeks after that, we finally slept together while his live-in girlfriend was out of town. Part of me felt like it was a double-jeopardy situation: I had already paid the price for sleeping with him, everybody thought it had already happened, so why shouldn't I at least get to actually do it? The other part of me knew that I wasn't taking his girlfriend into account. I haven't spoken to him since. I feel really sick about it.

Why do I keep putting myself in these situations? The only long-term serious relationship I've had was in college, during which I was cheated on extensively. When I think about it in a simple cost-benefit analysis structure, the Aaron thing seems downright absurd. The potential costs are so high—my relationship with my friend, this poor girl who is LIVING with Aaron, my own feelings—and the benefit is so low: The sex wasn't even good. Maybe when you're the one someone is cheating *with,* you're not putting yourself at risk in the same way you are when you're in a relationship. And some twisted part of my head/heart thinks if a guy is SO drawn to me that he's willing to risk his relationship, it must mean he feels really strongly. That drama is addictive. I even find myself rooting for budding potential affairs on TV shows I watch. Is that normal? WTF? All of this history has also served to make me incredibly cynical about men in general. They ALL seem to be cheaters, and I just don't think I can trust them—any of them.

I have trouble reconciling my behavior in my love life (and a general refusal to be vulnerable, admit feelings, appear weak) with the rest of my life. If you just struck out all the men, it would be clear that I'm a good person. I love and support my friends, I've dedicated myself to a career that I believe is changing the world for the better, and I'm close with my family. Why can't I act in my love life the way I do in the rest of my life?

I'm so tired of this life. I just want to be the person I *feel* like I am.

Always the Other Woman

—⚏—

Dear ATOW,

I believe that you're a good person. I can also tell from the tone of your letter that you've turned the corner from innocently saying, "Oh my god, why does this keep happening to me?" to "Why do I keep putting myself in these situations?" That's a start. But you still aren't taking full responsibility for your recklessness, your disregard for other women, and your willingness to cater to the needs of creepy, unethical guys.

I would suggest you lose the whole notion of "situations." You talk about it as if you're caught in these messy tar pits and helpless to pull yourself free. Every single time you *speak* to a guy who's involved with someone else, you're making a choice. And by taking things a step farther, you're *choosing* to grab exactly what you want without apology. So don't walk around telling these stories about how "one thing led to another" anymore. No one wants to hear your self-created, self-perpetuated narratives. You may not know a guy's girlfriend, and certainly he has more responsibility to that person than you do. But you're actively participating in something that's not just wrong; it's also terrible for you.

Where does the drama come from in these situations? It's stolen. The excitement and tension and secrecy are created at the expense of Aaron's girlfriend's trust and love for him. When you talk to him, all of the intensity there couldn't have *less* to do with you. It's drawn straight from his girlfriend's trust in him. He's getting a charge from sneaking around, NOT from you.

So instead of asking, "Why do I keep putting myself in these situations?" I think you need to ask, "Why do I choose to spend time with assholes and break their girlfriends' hearts?" Or, "Once I know a guy is a remorseless dick, why do I continue to speak to him?" "Why do I like hurting female strangers so much?" "Why do I have so little trouble disregarding the feelings of other people—my friend, my co-workers, etc.?"

I know I'm being harsh, but it's clear from your story about not speaking to your friend for a long time (after he had the audacity to be honest with you) that you've struggled to come to terms with your own responsibility, and your language—you "ended up" doing this or that, Aaron "seems to lack remorse," somehow men are untrustworthy but you're not—indicates that you still want to portray this as an ongoing tale that's only partially created by your choices.

You're not mysteriously falling into the same situation repeatedly. You only recognize interest when it has a faintly predatory intensity to it. What you need to know is that a lot of women find this intensity hugely *un*appealing. Some of us can feel this energy from across a football field. The narcissistic swagger of a cheater, with its undercurrents of anger and insecurity, is pretty unmistakable. I can befriend guys like that, but even if they're intellectually interesting, I can never take them seriously emotionally. They're never really putting their hearts on the line. It's like they're buying and selling sexual stocks constantly. Every move is a hedge. Their position is always covered.

I think you're playing a similar game in order to keep yourself protected and safe. For one thing, if you had closer relationships with women, you'd never wriggle your way into unavailable-man pants. You don't have enough real emotional intimacy in your life, so you're taking this strange shortcut to emotional intensity with taken men. You're substituting the electricity of sneaking around for rich, meaningful connections with people you can actually trust and lean on.

It's not that I don't understand how you might land there. I was pretty unethical at your age. I felt like I couldn't trust women, with their complicated needs and demands and judgments. I wanted to run around without considering whether I was stepping on some oversensitive girl's toes. I had an easy time writing off other women.

I bring this up because I think this is part of your puzzle. You don't have compassion for other women, because you don't have compassion for yourself. You're angry at yourself, so you take that anger out on other people. You're also very competitive, so when a guy gives you attention, you feel like you're "winning" somehow. We all grow up believing that only one of us can win—one beautiful princess at the ball, among all the goofy sidekicks and maiden aunts. So every time we're at a party, or a dinner, or a club, we organize the scene based on the same notion: Either we are the one who sparkles and thrills, or we're some dog in the corner. We're either the girl in the kitchen alcove, giggling and flirting, or the sad ignored girlfriend in the blurry background. We're either the white-hot sexy girl making out in the car or the sniffling loser girlfriend waiting around at home for her boyfriend to come back.

This isn't really winning. It's hurting yourself and hurting other women in one blow. It's serving your ass on a platter not to a prince but to a predator. It's feeding into everything sick and wrong about the blindest, least soulful dimensions of our culture. When you soak up the attentions of some smarmy creep, you're throwing away your compassion and your power and you're empowering that creep to pick a "winner." He's the one who determines which girl is superior and which girl is a sucker and which girl isn't worthy of his predatory gaze.

But do you know where the really strong, smart women are? They're in the other room, talking contentedly together. They would never in a million years let some dipshit with bad intentions offer them a false sense of superiority and intrigue just for being a shiny distraction from his girlfriend. And anyway, strong, empowered women are kryptonite to a guy like Aaron. You think he digs you because you're extra-sexy? He digs you because you're drawn in by his bullshit. He digs you because you're pretending. He digs you because you're just like him: strong on the outside, weak and needy on the inside.

Seducing guys is the easiest thing in the world, if that's what you really want to do. But don't tell yourself a story about how special you are just because you can lure a guy away from his girlfriend. That's not some special honor. It's embarrassing.

I can sense from your letter that at some level you already know these things. I'm shoving them in your face because you haven't yet reckoned with the ugliness of what you're choosing. You need to take a hard look at these things. Because it's not just about self-destructive behavior; it's about choosing to hurt other women and choosing to cater to a guy who's hurting other women. It's about STOMPING ON PEOPLE.

So why do you want to stomp on people? In addition to seeing men as cheaters, do you see women as only being out for themselves? Do you recognize how these characterizations are a projection of your own behavior? Do you see how your ruthlessness with yourself extends to other people? Do you see how your anger at yourself plays out? You're not just tempted to injure others; you feel that you're perfectly *entitled* to injure them. That you deserve it. That the world has fucked you over enough, and now you get to take whatever you want.

This goes beyond attraction or "situations" or even destructive behaviors. You're working out some deep-seated hurt in these scenarios. You have a lot to sort out. You need to quadruple the energy you put into your female friendships and pull way back on the social/romantic throttle. You need to talk honestly—not just with men, who I'm guessing are your primary cohort—about how confused and misguided and unfair you've been. You need to stop saying, "Why does this always happen?" and start saying, "I am never fucking doing THAT again, that's for sure."

So this is the end of one part of your story. The cheaters chapter is officially over.

At the end of the chapter, you are ragged and wrecked. You feel ashamed, and that makes you angry. You feel like everyone misunderstands you and blames you for things that aren't your fault. You feel lonely. You're tired of having to figure this stuff out all by yourself. You just want a little help, for once, instead of always having to go it alone.

You may wonder, without the excitement, without the drama of the forbidden guy, what is there? Stay with that thought. Stay with the messy aftermath. Imagine yourself at a party, *not* sparkling. Imagine losing. Imagine being small and sorrowful and admitting how little you really know. Imagine saying the wrong thing and feeling awkward, over and over again. This messiness, this pain, this void, are where real strength and happiness begin. Forget seduction and intrigue. Talk to the other women at a party. Then go home and take a bath and feel good about sticking to your principles and being the honorable person you really are, deep inside.

Polly

That Bitter Aftertaste

Dear Polly,

I'm a thirty-two-year-old single woman. I love my life—my friends, my job, the city in which I live. I have a creative outlet and I exercise and I have a lot of passion for living. But inside I have a problem with bitterness. I feel bitter every single day. I can't stop thinking about the men who have hurt me, and I think about at least two or three of them every day (not always the same ones), sometimes during the day, but mostly at night when I'm trying to fall asleep. I think about when things were good and then how they hurt me, and I wonder why they didn't love me, and I imagine what I would say to them if I saw them again, and then I tumble into a stony feeling of grit, of wanting to be invulnerable. I have a physical response to these emotions: My chest hurts, my stomach hurts, and the pain stretches out to my fingertips. I lose my breath in the pain. I sometimes wonder if in some way I actually enjoy this awful feeling, just because it's feeling something in my heart. But I fear that it will make me sick in the long run. I feel like it's gonna give me cancer or ulcers just to think these sad, echoing thoughts every day.

I don't want to be bitter, and I don't want to be that friend everyone feels sorry for because she's perpetually single, but that's what I'm turning into. When things do go well with a guy, I am able to forget about my past pain and let myself believe in a future with someone I like, if cautiously. But it never works out, and I don't know why. I'm not clingy or high-maintenance; I like who I am and what I'm doing with my life; I have my own life but I want to share it with someone, and I just keep getting hurt. With the last two guys I dated, I actually felt that elusive "click" of feeling connected to someone and like I could be myself with them, and being able to see myself with them for a long time, which hasn't happened in ages, but it turned out that neither of them were interested in trying a long-term relationship with me. And I don't know how many instances of the death of hope I can take or how many men will fit in my Rolodex of Men Who've Made Me Bitter.

It's getting really, really hard to keep getting out there and trying and to stay positive and open about myself and about men. I'm sick of convincing/allowing myself to let go and be vulnerable and then being crushed in the end, and I'm sick of feeling this nightly blank emptiness punctuated by the stabbing emotional pain of bitterness. I haven't had a real boyfriend in over five years. I'm tired and I'm lonely and I'm beginning to feel like a ghost. How can I stop obsessing over the people who have hurt me, and how can I move forward in my romantic life without fear or, worse, apathy? Thanks for your help.

Signed,
Alone Again, Naturally

—⟋⟍—

Dear AAN,

The first thing you need to know—understand, believe, breathe in—is that there is nothing wrong with you. There. Is. Nothing. Wrong. With. You. The guys who hurt you, the guys who don't want to date you: These people are irrelevant. They are not your mother. They are not your father or your sister or your best friend. Compared to your parents, your friends, they are nothing—flies in the room, cockroaches in the cupboard.

Nothing. Fixating on them is like fixating on marrying George Clooney. They are irrelevant.

So why do they feel relevant to you? Because you BELIEVE that there's something wrong with you, and you're trying to figure out what it is. That belief is what's wrong with you.

Every night you pray to the gods of rejection. Your prayer ritual involves replaying the past, loading one reel after another, footage of men who broke your heart, as if that's romantic or special, getting your heart broken. Meanwhile, those guys—like so many—were probably just allergic to emotion or seriousness of purpose or vulnerability. I'm not being a dick about it; ask any man and he'll back me up. Maybe they simply weren't mature enough to handle you or anyone else. And yet the reel footage seems dramatic; the mystery seems compelling. How did you screw it all up? What did you do to turn them away? The problem lies somewhere in you, not in them. They were rational, intelligent beings whose rejections said something important about what's screwed up about you. If only you could figure out what it was!

Cobbling together a string of rejections by men and trying to make sense of them is like trying to read tea leaves. Why? Because single men have many, many allergies.

Most single men are gluten-sensitive, lactose-intolerant, asthmatic mutants. They can't tolerate wheat or soy or fleeting glimpses of heaviness. When they sense substance, regrets, high stakes, potential long-term entanglements, concern, interest, a pulse, they flee in terror like neurotic dogs in the presence of teetering lamps. The smallest change in weather, the tiniest shift in cabin pressure, the most minuscule adjustment in tone or mood, sends them running.

It's not personal. It's not even interesting. It's certainly not the stuff of mystery, nothing to build a lifelong religion around. YOU ARE CURRENTLY PRAYING AT THE ALTAR OF THE MOST TEDIOUS RELIGION IN THE UNIVERSE.

(I'm not shaming you! Sweet Christ in high heaven almighty, NO. I understand. Every single woman reading this understands!) Go ask a man what he thinks about another man having rejected you. He'll snort like even contemplating it for half a second demeans both of you. If you push it, he'll say maybe the guy met someone on the subway, or maybe he had a bad reaction to some mussels, and then he didn't feel like explaining it, or maybe he was bored. Guys assume that other guys are indifferent unless they have explicit proof otherwise.

So should you.

Instead of digging into the reasons for this state of affairs, instead treating it as your personal fucking responsibility to root out the problem and eradicate it, instead of redoubling your efforts to be more lovable and better, always approaching some infinite ideal of the whip-smart but easygoing professional with a body like a fuck doll, you need to take a good look at yourself and accept what you see. When it comes to love, at least, you must try to stop being or seeming "better." You need to accept exactly who you are and stop wishing it would change, that you'd be more palatable to the masses. "I am a reasonably good-looking woman with a tendency to cry at the drop of a hat." "I am opinionated and impatient, and I have a bad habit of fixating on stuff I don't understand." "I am bored by most people, and I wish I had the money and the space to own llamas."

When I finally decided to stop seeming cooler and more easygoing than I actually was, when I finally stopped pretending that nothing bothered me, that I didn't need to talk about heavy stuff or express my emotions, when I finally stopped seeing tears as a weakness (being utterly unable to cry is a pretty blatant weakness, if you ask me), that's when I realized that I was trying to truss up my weird in a shiny conventional package. Guys always thought I was a Little Debbie snack cake, but then they'd open the package and find anchovies and feel disappointed. Instead of questioning why I was spending time with guys who only craved fluff and sugar, I grew ashamed of my oily, salty nature. I tried to act sweeter, snackier, Littler.

Anchovies don't have the easiest time imitating Ho Hos. If you ever want to go insane, try behaving like something you're not. At my lowest points, I was (unconsciously) committed to repressing all ME-ness and approximating what I saw as my current boyfriend's ideal woman. Needless to say, I was not convincing at this charade. But I didn't even know that I was acting! I thought I was just trying to be less *wrong,* less *bad,* less *crazy.*

Why did I believe these things about myself? Because I often went out with men who liked me because I was semi-attractive and smart and funny. I often attracted these men by pouring on the charm, appearing nonchalant, appearing devil-may-care. My goal was to mask the fact that I was an extremely emotional, thoughtful, moody, obnoxious, demanding anchovy. These boyfriends wanted to make it work because they wanted a semi-attractive, smart, funny girlfriend, not because they wanted ME.

As long as you aim to please men, you don't. The second you decide to please yourself, guess what? Everybody wants a slice of that action. I'll never forget, right after I vowed to stop settling for mediocre, half-interested men (even if it meant becoming a dog lady, which suddenly seemed sort of appealing), I went to this wedding and I was mobbed by guys. I could finally see clearly that half of them just wanted to sleep with me and weren't looking for anything serious. The other half was deluded into thinking I was super-fun and easygoing around the clock (um, no), and that seemed like a great kind of a girlfriend to have. Maybe one of them was actually into me, but he was wrong in thinking that we'd be good together. I could see that. It was like that moment where the kid who's never heard a single sound before fires up his cochlear implant for the first time. My sudden ability to see attraction and rejection as a mere matter of appetite and taste and misinformation transformed my view of the world.

Strangely, everything started to pulsate with possibility! You'd think that marching around saying, "Oh, we wouldn't work. I'm way too bossy for you," might feel a little pessimistic, but instead it felt liberating. I was curious but detached until I could get more information. I wanted to fall in love with someone. That was my goal, and I wasn't shy about saying so. But I needed to see a real hunger for anchovies, to the point where nothing else would do.

So first, you have to break your bad nightly habit. But you must be totally committed to cutting this shitty religion of yours off at the knees. Before you go to bed at night, I want you to write down at least three things you're grateful for. They could be people, or places, or experiences. If you think of more, write those down, too. Then I want you to write down at least two things you did that day that you're proud of. If you didn't do anything that impressive, just write down something you did that was really just pure YOU. Maybe you made up a song about armpits, or ate two Cronuts in one sitting, or ran four miles and then watched a really stupid episode of *CSI: Barcelona*. Notice that you get credit for doing the so-called wrong thing, like napping, or eating butter bombs, or crying over a really good performance on *So You Think You Can Dance*.

You are going to fall in love with what you have and fall in love with who you are. Do not take the so-called bad or wrong things about you, that boyfriends or men or even women have told you, and try to "get rid" of those things. Put that stuff on the list right next to the stuff you're proud of. "Cried after hearing the 'Hugs Are Fun' song on *Yo Gabba Gabba!*" "Slipped on the stairs and wondered if my landlord thought I was drunk, then craved a drink." "Bailed on the dinner party and made mac and cheese out of a box instead, and it was awesome."

Your bitterness is caused by the notion that these men form one all-powerful, critical OZ that thinks you're not good enough. Everything you do during the day backs this up. You are rejectable. Look at how you fuck things up. Look how not cute enough you are. Look how grumpy. Look how not attractive your attitude can be.

You have to quiet the bad OZ voices, during the day and at night. Stop pushing back against a phantom. You are not a ghost; this creation of yours is. Maybe it's an echo of something from your childhood. Maybe it's just a bad cognitive habit you've had for a while. If it helps to map out a life alone—what could make that look better, look okay?—then do it. For me, I needed to think that if I didn't find the right man, I'd definitely be pouring my time into crazy interesting things. I would learn to sew my own clothes and paint. I would adopt fifteen dogs. I would write poetry on the walls of my dining room. Instead of being afraid of getting "weird" and "lonely," I needed to believe that I would engage with the world, create things, reveal myself to others as a serious freak without shame, and just generally throw myself into the world with abandon.

But I also respect your interest in sharing your life. Most of us feel the same way.

But you MUST stop fucking yourself over with this lazy, self-destructive nightly habit of yours. Do the things you need to do (show up to work, exercise, be good to your friends), and otherwise give yourself exactly what you need to be happy, and do not punish yourself for a second. Give yourself love and attention and respect. Treat your thoughts and feelings like the precious gems that they are. Respect yourself enough to allow yourself to be stubborn, shy, recalcitrant, angry, confused. Forgive yourself for this Bitter Era, but proclaim that it's over. Today, it ends. Buy a pretty notebook for your gratitude and your self-acceptance, and put it by the bed. Dare to believe that this could change you. Don't be cynical. Don't go through the motions with this. The Bitter Era is done. You are celebrating yourself now, who you are RIGHT NOW, not a week from now, not a year from now. You are looking for someone with a taste for you, and nothing less will do. Believe that there is someone who fits that description. Believe that you deserve it, you deserve to be loved. It's all going to work out just fine.

And when you finally find the right person for you, it will feel effortless. It will feel right. It won't be perfect, but it will still be worlds apart from these other relationships you've had. But you know what? You won't be surprised. Because once you build your own religion around gratitude and pride in who you are, at your best *and* at your worst, you'll feel better than you ever have before. It will only seem natural for people to want to be closer to you.

Look around you, the way you're living now. Commit it to memory. Because everything is about to change.

Polly

IV

Weepiness Is Next to Godliness

Drunk No More

Dear Polly,

I feel I'm at a transitional period in my life, straddling the line between messed-up party girl and responsible woman. For most of my early twenties, I rarely went more than a few days sober, and my life essentially revolved around nonstop drinking and sex. Up until a few months ago, I was drifting into "real problem" territory, and I'm currently not imbibing. Not only that, but I have been treating my body well by working out, eating right, and quitting smoking. It feels great. But not drinking (and smoking) also means that I have to deal with my pesky insecurities head-on. There's always a voice in the back of my mind telling me that this new life is great, but it would be so much easier to slip back into that boozy oblivion. I feel like I'm transitioning into a true "responsible adult" life, but I'm terrified of this voice that seems to want me to fail. Nothing scares me more than giving in and going back to who I used to be, yet part of me feels it's inevitable (even though I have complete control over the situation).

Another problem with having all this raw emotion is that . . . well, I feel raw. Suddenly I'm seeing glaring intimacy issues I never even knew I had. It's easy to feel a connection (and sleep with someone) after a bottle of wine, but now I find myself shying away from men who want nothing more than to adore me. They're always respectful, but I still find myself frozen in discomfort when things move beyond a chaste kiss or they send me a sappy message. Sometimes this aversion even turns to mild disgust, and I've ended things with a few guys who "liked me too much." (It shouldn't be surprising that my last few serious relationships were with guys who did a great job of stringing me along.)

How do I convince myself not only that I am better off without the booze numbing my life but that I'm worthy of the decent guys who have come with this new lifestyle? I can't go back to the way things were before, but I'm almost afraid not to.

Almost Adult

—❦—

Dear Almost Adult,

You have to find the beauty in the rawness you're feeling and the sweetness that lies just beyond your discomfort at being watched and appreciated and loved. It's natural that you would push these unfamiliar feelings away. You're much more familiar with a very different kind of joy, a joy that comes from blurring the world enough that you can be a blaring loudspeaker, a spinning top, a gorgeous automated toy. That's boozy carnival-ride joy for you: You get to blurt out the craziest shit, toss back another drink, take your clothes off, and you never have to notice any of the pain or fragility underneath it all. The whole world is a hazy kaleidoscope of carpe diem recklessness.

Being a drunk twentysomething woman who's up for any flavor of fun can feel like being the Mother of Dragons from *Game of Thrones*. You go wherever you want, you take whatever you want, you don't care who doesn't like it. You can't hear the voices, inside you or outside you, that want you to fail. You're too busy dancing and drinking and yelling, "I AM THE BLOOD OF THE DRAGON."

And let's be honest, drunken grandiosity has its appeal. There are times when that existence feels exhilarating and wild and, frankly, superior to the anxious control that calm, sober people have to exert over their lives. Drinking sometimes seems to offer a quick, temporary exit from feeling blah, particularly when you're drinking to handle an underlying depression, which I think might be the case for you. That makes it really tough to prefer sober clarity. Because instead of sanity and happiness and ambition when you're sober, what *you* get are disparaging voices and melancholy and aimlessness. How will you find your path to happiness *that* way? Why be sober at all?

Here's why: Because if you go back to the bottle and keep escaping into your blurry merry-go-round world, you'll never learn or grow. Learning and growing aren't *just* about accepting the company of men who like you for more than your twirling, dizzy self. It's also about feeling the weight of melancholy press on you in a new, helpful way. That kind of sadness isn't a fleeting feeling to stomp out; it's something more sublime. It allows you to really notice the people around you, to recognize the pain they carry with them, to see the pureness of their hearts. The sad thing about recovering from addiction is that you still equate rawness with weakness, failure, collapse. But rawness is life! With rawness comes the promise of overcoming a bleak, hazy depression and stepping into the sunshine, where you can see yourself without judgment, where you hear the world at normal volume, and where you actually connect with people.

It's crazy that coolness—that kind of willful indifference that's associated with boozing—is something so many of us covet. Sexiness is all too often *defined* as disinterest, the attitude of someone who barely sees us at all. All too often we tell ourselves that we feel more alive when we're striving to be noticed. As long as a guy isn't looking at you and you're craving his attention, you don't have to think about who or what you are.

But the respectful, adoring energy you describe in the sober men around you—that energy is so much more promising in the long term. Once you give in to it, that's the energy of poetry, of art, of life-bending happiness. It's the energy of a partner who's a great lover and a dependable friend and a good listener. It sounds corny, but trust me, *that* is what you want. I'm not saying find yourself any fawning guy and settle down. I'm saying don't turn your back on positive attention from someone sane just because it makes you uncomfortable. Be patient, take a deep breath, and try to train yourself to tolerate positive attention for a change.

Remember, you only find that kind of adoring energy repellent because you hate being seen clearly, because at some level, you hate yourself. You only back away from it because you want to back away from yourself. You don't want a crystal clear, high-definition mirror. You want to spot your smeary reflection in the side of a napkin holder, four beers into an afternoon bender. You want to be a sexy, indifferent blur, because then you're never still enough to notice that you're disappointing to yourself, that you're depressed, that you're running from the truth.

Before you can tolerate sobriety and the attentions of sober men, you have to learn to tolerate looking into that crystal clear, high-definition mirror. You have to look at yourself and see someone who's *not* invincible or unfailingly sexy.

You are weak and raw and broken, and that's okay. That's where real life begins. Throw yourself into that rawness. Dive into a bunch of stories about absorbing and leaning into disappointment and loss and melancholy as a way of moving through it. Go watch *Living Out Loud* or *Eternal Sunshine of the Spotless Mind* or *Sex, Lies, and Videotape*. Read *The Wind-Up*

Bird Chronicle by Haruki Murakami. Read *Angle of Repose* by Wallace Stegner. Read *The Sheltering Sky* by Paul Bowles. Read *Mating* by Norman Rush. Being raw means connecting to other people's trials and noticing how we all have to find our own answers; we all have to learn how to show up and breathe without grasping for something to deliver us from our own pain. When you resist your own rawness and pain, you only create more pain for yourself.

You have to make peace with yourself. Push away the bad voices, again and again, and replace them with something kinder and more patient. Say to yourself, "I'm broken right now, but I'm doing my best." Take in the electricity, the shivers, the rough-hewn fear of your raw state, and eventually, if you welcome these feelings in enough without fighting them, you'll find inspiration and comfort there. Let this crisis guide you to higher ground.

Polly

I'm Dating My Best Friend's Ex

Dear Polly,

I've committed the cardinal friendship sin of dating the ex-boyfriend of one of my closest friends. I did this knowing that their breakup had been devastating for her, and understandably she feels betrayed and disgusted.

Their relationship ended about ten years ago, when we were in college (we're in our early thirties now), and we all lived in separate cities until recently, when he moved to mine. He didn't know many people in town, so I invited him to various social events, which developed from casual friendship into mutually romantic feelings.

In an effort to handle it in the best way possible, I was immediately honest with my friend (despite our distance and the hypothetical ease of duplicity). In my mind, since the relationship had occurred so long ago, I wasn't choosing between the two. I naively imagined that I would tell the friend and she would initially be hurt but ultimately forgive me.

It's been a few months, and aside from a few painful text and e-mail exchanges she wants nothing to do with me. She is not okay with the relationship and does not envision returning to our prior friendship.

I have always validated and supported her feelings throughout our friendship, but it's tricky in this case, because in doing so, I condemn myself. In case it is relevant, I know that she struggles with depression or possibly manic depression.

Should I resign myself to losing a close friend because of the romantic choice that I made and simply do my best to nurture my other friendships? I know that friendships end frequently for less dramatic reasons. But I value our history and her beautiful brain and jokes and spirit and of course don't want that outcome.

Or should I continue reaching out to this friend, in hopes that her feelings will evolve? In the latter case, to what degree/in what format can I do so without feeling like a stalker (or like I'm patronizing her, as in "Are you over this yet?")? Thus far, it has felt as though I can't say anything right.

I've communicated that I want to be her friend and work things out, but that's actually considered to be MORE hurtful, because in addition to dating her ex, I am inadvertently blaming the end of our friendship on her.

As far as the relationship is concerned, I don't regret anything (aside, obviously, from causing pain for a loved one). I've never had the luxury of dating a friend and, though it's early, have never been in a relationship so mutually respectful, positive, and honest. He even reads me Ask Polly columns aloud while I'm driving!

Any suggestions you can offer as a sage and objective party would be greatly appreciated.

Signed,
Fearful of a Lifelong Rift

—⟋⟍—

Dear FOALR,

Okay, I have to admit, you got me right where you want me with that last bit. He reads you Ask Polly columns aloud while you're driving? DO NOT LET GO OF THIS BEAUTI-FUL MAN.

So, look. No matter where you fall on the scale from "Never, ever date the ex of a close friend!" to "Do whatever you want with whomever you want, true love will prevail in the end!" the fact remains that you made a choice. You may have assumed that everything would be fine once you told your friend about your choice, but you chose to take that risk. You didn't call her to see how she felt BEFORE you went for it with your guy, thereby valuing the friendship over your brand-new love match. You were not willing to hear "No, I don't want you dating him. That would upset me." You chose him over her.

And you are *still* choosing him over her. Maybe that's exactly as it should be. Maybe you two are the perfect pair, and a long-term friendship can't possibly measure up to this romance. Maybe you will die in this guy's arms sixty years from now, and you'll thank your lucky stars that you put him first.

No one is going to tell you you're a huge asshole for choosing love in this case. It's been a decade since he dated your friend. He lives in your town; she lives far away. But honestly, it was a mistake not to call her first, even if you were going to kiss the guy either way. It was a mistake. You sent a clear message with that mistake. Your priorities were clear.

For your friend, this situation is heartbreaking. Don't bring her manic depression into it. Don't say to yourself, "She should let go of this; they dated ten years ago." Don't say, "If she weren't THE WAY SHE IS—oversensitive, depressed, lonely—she'd be cool with this. I mean, what's the big deal? It's not like they were ever getting back together. He never loved her the way he loves me. He says so himself! He always felt like there was something missing there."

Do you see what's happening? Do you see how you win and she loses? Put yourself in your friend's shoes and crawl into her mind. BE HER for a minute now. Imagine that the two people you've loved and trusted the most in the world are now aligning themselves and discussing you thoroughly and then leaving you out of all of it and moving forward without you. You don't have to be manic-depressive or have an overactive imagination to picture that. Can you understand that? Imagine it. They want each other, not you. You're not important anymore. You don't matter. They made their choice. They win and you lose. When he dumped you, you were crushed, and your friend knew all about that. But she went for it anyway. She didn't call you first. She didn't check in. If she had just *talked* to you, you could've thought it over and maybe even given her your blessing. That would've felt so much better, even if you had mixed feelings. You might not have liked it, but you would've known that she cared enough about you not to want to fuck over your friendship.

But she didn't do that. And not only that, now you have this feeling, no matter how you try to fight it, that she is better than you. You've wished that things would've worked out with your ex so many times, but you were never good enough for him. That's how it felt. And now *she* is good enough. Your friend! She wins his heart! And you don't matter. You are nothing.

I know you think I'm being a little dramatic about this. And honestly, I don't give a flying fuck who dates or marries or makes babies with any of my exes anymore. Take them all! I can hardly even imagine caring anymore, and I understand why people say, "Whatever, get over it, move on," when it comes to situations like these.

I'm not saying you're a bad person. Not remotely. All I'm saying is this: You cannot fathom the psychic turmoil you've incited with this very casual, Nothing to Do with Her decision. You can't touch how big this is for her. Even if you struggle to understand—and I *do* think you're trying—you can't touch it. So first of all, trust me there. Open your mind as wide as it can go and honor the fact that she is in real pain, and your choice not to consult her is at the center of that pain. You made your choice, and you chose him. Say that out loud and own it. This wasn't a casual mistake, actually. You actively chose him over her.

When I was twenty-six years old, I was in love with someone great and I had a great job and I was reasonably happy. I was a mess in many ways, but I was sallying forth with my life. One day, my very best friend in the whole world sat me down and told me that she had been sleeping with my ex, who was my second-best friend in the world. My ex had dumped me six years earlier. I always had the sense that he was looking for someone *better than me*. He was extremely smart and attractive and talented. I always felt like I was less amazing than him—or that, at the very least, he didn't recognize that I was just as amazing as he was. It drove me nuts. But we were good friends! I loved him.

But you know who I loved the most? My best friend. I loved her like I've never loved any other female friend, before or since. We felt like the most in-love straight women ever to have lived. We were together all the time, the way you can only be together when you're twenty-six years old and living in the giant upscale hipster mall that is San Francisco. We marched through the fog in our black boots like a two-headed, four-legged Bay City cliché, smoking American Spirit Lights and high-fiving over stupid jokes and eating giant falafels and drinking pints of Guinness and finishing each other's sentences and laughing and feeling seen and heard and understood completely for the first time. I'm making us sound terrible, but we weren't so bad most of the time.

No one understood me the way she did. And I admired her so much. I laughed at all her jokes. I was a huge fan. (I would never use that word with anyone else.) We cried together. We were very self-protective people who let down our guard with each other because that part seemed fated somehow. It was like we were supposed to tell each other the truth. Sometimes I felt small in her presence, because she was so big. But looking back, we were both big, and we both felt smaller than each other sometimes.

We were young and confused, and the whole thing was complicated. We didn't know how to sort through our problems. We should've followed the rules of love relationships: Respect the other person's feelings, don't always lead with what YOU need, give the other person some room, and address what they say with an open heart. I know that I was bad at those things back then.

And maybe we were already falling apart as friends when this happened. Even so, when she started dating my ex, it was like some cruel god reached down and took my two most important, most trusted friends and ripped them away from me. I had nothing, and they had everything.

Let me be clear: When she first told me, over lunch, I was fine with it. I said, "Oh, that's funny. No, it makes sense that you two would be together." He had always had a little crush on her; I knew that. And then I mentioned it to my roommate, and he said, "Oh, they've been dating for a while now. *Everyone* knows that. They would kiss when you walked out of the room."

The disrespect of that! That the two people I loved the most would sneak around behind my back. And when I confronted them about it, they both said, "I thought he/she should tell you, since you two were closer than I was with you." They BOTH undervalued my friendship!

The aftermath was a terrible mess. I was angry. My ex was avoidant about discussing it, and then he'd gripe about her to me, and then he'd turn around and tell her things I told him. My friend was apologetic, then defensive, then hostile, then she just cut me off completely. Then she'd get mad at my ex for agreeing to have lunch with me when I came to town. And

I was also apologetic, defensive, hostile. I talked shit to a lot of people, and so did they. It was a giant ball of shit.

I wish I'd just stepped back and dealt with it on my own, like your friend is doing. I tried to do that, but I was too weak. I had no compass. I was so hurt. Even when I was talking to one or the other of them very openly about how I felt, even when I was trying to listen and understand either one of them, there was a voice in my head saying, "YOU DON'T MATTER TO THEM. THEY CHOSE EACH OTHER OVER YOU. YOU ARE LESS THAN THEM. YOU ARE NOTHING."

I know that makes me sound like a crazy person. All I can say in my defense is that I was so vulnerable with each of them, and then they were gone, and I was devastated, and it was harder than any simple breakup I've ever experienced. My past with my ex felt like it was stolen out of my hands. He had never been mine. She was never mine. Part of my history was lost, somehow.

We are all friends now, almost twenty years later. But we never went back to what we were—not even close. I love them both and I went to both of their weddings (to different people) and I was so glad to be there. I don't feel inferior anymore, obviously, and I have to dig a little to remember that sensation, honestly. But this one event, the way it was handled and the fallout from it, changed everything.

I know that my situation and your situation are very different. But you write, "I have always validated and supported her feelings throughout our friendship, but it's tricky in this case, because in doing so, I condemn myself." How do her hurt feelings condemn you, exactly? You hurt her. That's a fact. Can you accept that? If you can't admit that you made a choice, and it was a choice that hurt her more than you can possibly imagine, then you're probably right to assume that there is no friendship there.

But you don't have to be right, do you? You don't have to

look at what you did and say, "I didn't do anything wrong. I was right to go for it," do you? Because that's not true. Is it not enough to get the guy; you also have to be right, too? You also have to be blameless? That's a lot to ask, don't you think?

Listen to me: You were WRONG. You should've talked to your friend first. Even if you weren't going to honor or respect her feelings, you should've talked to her first. You can hear someone out and still make your own choices. That would've made all the difference, I'm guessing. You made a mistake.

It's not the end of the world. But it might be the end of your friendship.

If you really do care about her, you should throw yourself into a state of empathy for where she is right now. That's not condescending; that's being a human being with a heart who cares a lot. Ask your new boyfriend to join you in that state. Focus on her beautiful brain and jokes and spirit and how crumpled and hurt she feels now. Tell her you're sorry for not telling her as soon as you considered getting together with him. Tell her you didn't think it through enough or try it on for size and if you were in her shoes, you'd be incredibly hurt, too. Tell her you're sorry. Tell her that you understand why she's mad and you would be mad, too, but you will never stop wanting to be her friend. You want her in your life. You want to know her until you're both old and gray. You love her and you miss her.

Keep saying those things. She'll either come around or she won't, but if you really care, don't give up. Keep sticking your neck out and being true to your friendship. Accepting that you made a mistake and you were wrong to handle this the way you did: This is a crucial first step to growing up and becoming a stronger, better person. Above all, never, ever say to yourself or to your new guy or to anyone else, "She should be over this by now." That's not fair. You don't know how it feels. You may try to imagine it—that's a step! But you don't know. Painting someone as weak or pathetic for feeling hurt or overwhelmed or heartbroken is inexcusable. It's antihuman. This world is filled with people who think feeling less, being indifferent, makes you strong. Don't believe that. Be one of the smart, thoughtful people who stands up for sensitive people. When you stand up for sensitive, hurt people, you're also standing up for vulnerability and authenticity and true love.

Whether she ever speaks to you again or not, that's her choice. I will say that I did eventually learn to stop defining my ex-boyfriends as MINE. The carelessness I encountered from those two was instructive. You can love someone like crazy, but it does actually matter how much they love you back. It says something about my maturity level that I ignored their feelings, good and bad, and defined the world based on my own little bubble of experience.

What bothers me, though, even now, is that we never got it all back—the love we shared, the bond the three of us had, together and separately. We're still old friends who talk every year or so. We love each other. But what we had is lost.

Some people really *are* irreplaceable—who they are, your history together, the way you feel when you're together. I have old friends today with whom I very deliberately tackled a mountain of trouble because I knew that if I ever dumped them or let things fall apart, they were sure to become ghosts. (Mind you, I have other friendships that ended and didn't leave a hole at all, and I knew they wouldn't.)

If you know that she will become a ghost and she'll haunt you? If you know that she's that special? Apologize as much as it takes. Don't stalk her, but don't give up. Check in every few months and say, "I still care and I won't stop caring." If she tells you to fuck off forever, send her a note a year later and say you're still sorry, you still love her, you're still there for her if she ever comes around. Admit that you chose him over her.

That was understandable. That was your choice. But the way you went about it was wrong. Admit that, too.

Early, formative close friendships are special. Don't shrug this off if you really do care. It will be hard to handle her anger. It will also help you to grow. You might feel like a real asshole sometimes, but you're not an asshole. You just made a mistake. Even so, if you don't acknowledge that your small mistake feels huge to her, if you can't sit in the company of her pain and take it in and accept it, then you're making an even bigger mistake—for her and for yourself. This is an empathy test. This is a lesson in maturity. This is the way toward a bigger, more generous heart.

Polly

How Do I Get Over This Betrayal?

Dear Polly,

In 2009, I married the man I never thought I'd meet: the man I actually WANTED to marry and have children with and spend the rest of my life being loved by and loving. I was thirty-nine. Six months later, I was pregnant with our son, and six months after that he was informing me that we needed to separate.

During months four and five of my pregnancy, he'd been recalled to active duty with the Coast Guard to help with the BP oil spill in the Gulf, and while he was there, he was the same loving, doting man I'd known for five years. Once he returned, he was different: not coming to bed with me, going on walks or running errands that lasted for hours, and, most hurtful of all, announcing that he was taking a weekend trip to Boston, then, after not being in touch all weekend, texting me to let me know he was really sick and wouldn't be returning the night he was supposed to. Which of course made me extremely concerned, then infuriated when I discovered that he was hungover, not sick. He had missed our final Lamaze class and seemed to feel no qualms about it.

In the meantime, the horrible fights had started. I was concerned about the dramatic change in his personality and actions, and after several mumblings about working it out on his own, he finally blew up at me one night, essentially scream-ing about everything I'd ever done wrong the entire time we'd known each other. Now, our relationship was certainly not perfect, and in hindsight (of course) I can see that we'd let our communication—for which we'd always been the envy of our friends—get lazy because we took it for granted. However, this blowup took me completely off guard. Forget that I was already emotional and hopped-up on pregnancy hormones. I was completely taken aback.

Fast-forward through the pregnancy (all the while he was awful, sending me horrific e-mails trying to get me to make a decision about our unborn son's custody and visitation arrangement, all the while insisting he wasn't thinking about divorce), through the first awful, completely sleep-deprived months of having a brand-new baby while not knowing what was going on with my marriage, and through two years of lawyer negotiations, to our eventual divorce, which was finalized two years ago. I still haven't been able to forgive him.

I'm not pining or hoping for reconciliation. That ship sailed long ago and was cemented when I discovered that he met someone in Louisiana. Who, interestingly, was from Boston. Which everyone else probably saw coming from a mile away, but I did not. At any rate, while we are civil for the sake of our son (who is four now and adores his daddy, and I wouldn't want that any other way), I can't seem to finally let this massive betrayal go. I'm dating, sort of, but haven't connected with anyone and am thinking it's just ME and am afraid I'm never going to be able to trust anyone ever again. I've been to therapy with two different people, and while they've been great cheerleaders, their advice boils down to "Just do it." If it's an ass kicking that I need, I'll take it; I am just desperately exhausted from the anger and the feeling of injustice and would love to be rid of it.

Want to Be a Better, Happier Mom

—◊◊◊—

Dear WTBABHM,

When someone is wrong for you, he's just wrong for you. Things fall apart. There's no way to hold it together. You can't be nicer or better or sexier. You can't make him more patient or more caring or more loyal. Nothing about this is your fault. And let me just say that men who fall in love with other women while their partners are pregnant are not exactly the tippity top of the heap in most guides to common human varietals.

But let's not barrel down that rageful road. Instead, I think you need to survey the facts on the ground and see that you just dodged a major bullet. That guy was never going to give you the support and love that you deserve, ever. My guess is that he's not capable of sticking by someone's side when the chips are down. Some people are like that. They love the hell out of you one minute, but as soon as the situation shifts—they get bored, you get pregnant—they're out. I'll bet that if you roll back the tape, you'll see a few different examples of him backing away from you.

In fact, your letter offers a pretty informative lesson for other women out there who wonder whether or not they can really lean on their partners and trust them to see them through the rough road ahead. If a guy seems to love you yet his behaviors show an interest in creating greater and greater distance, if he never takes responsibility for anything he says or does, backs away when you need him most, or seems unable or unwilling to get to the bottom of any conflict with you? You shouldn't marry that guy. A lot of people—not just men—are terrible at making room for another human being in their lives. If you're dating someone who pulls away even as your bond should be strengthening, that's doesn't bode well. Don't sign up for a lifetime of that. So many people do.

I know that it's incredibly hard to raise your son alone while dealing with this betrayal. The structure of your day-to-day life is a regular reminder of the trauma you experienced at the hands of your ex. It's easy to see why his shitty behavior might scare you away from dipping a toe into the dating pool again.

But it's time to rid yourself of the aftertaste of his bad decisions once and for all. His choices don't define you. His heartlessness and lack of loyalty have nothing to do with you. That's who he is. You didn't write that story. It's time to stop being the woman who got left behind when she was pregnant and be someone else instead.

I'm not saying you need to clamp down on your emotions. I'm just saying that it's a mistake—one that's unfortunately common among women—to let some guy's shitty decisions form part of your lasting identity. You have to make sure to define your life story in a new way.

I don't think the challenge for you is to simply try to get over that betrayal and learn to trust in love again. I think your challenge is to reinvent your whole life so that it looks beautiful whether or not it has a man in it. If you start dating right now, I think you're going to feel traumatized. You need to be stronger and healthier and happier before you date again. You're sitting around asking, "How do I do this?" as if finding another man is the logical next step. Your therapists are saying, "DO IT! GO FOR IT!" and I think that points to a central misconception of where you are and what you need.

It's okay to want love in your life. But your letter suggests that you don't feel ready for love yet. You don't feel worthy of love yet. You still feel like someone who got dumped on her ass. The path from here doesn't involve dating (to magically make it all better), and it doesn't involve finding some kind of closure with your ex (who needs to be permanently filed under "MR. WRONG" and who you're right not to reconsider for a second). The path from here is all about you and you alone: the things that bring you happiness and make you feel strong and independent. What are those things?

Where do you turn when no one is picking up the phone?

How do you take care of yourself? What makes you feel like you're on the right track? What makes you forget about your ex and dating and men in general?

Let's try this: If I told you that you would never, ever fall in love again, what kind of a plan would you make to ensure your own happiness moving forward? What would you work toward? What would you do more of? I bet that you'd have to give up on some big dreams that you care about a lot. But I also bet that giving up some of those things might add up to a weird kind of freedom. Maybe you'd cut your hair short and save up for a house. Maybe you'd start riding horses or writing poetry or growing sunflowers or taking dance lessons or baking pies.

Instead of seeing your balance of days on earth as either a sad, lonely slog through single motherhood or a rosy daydream thanks to some magical second marriage, you need to begin by painting a picture that doesn't include love. You need to stop making room in your life for someone else's love and start making room for yourself instead. When you feel proud of yourself and care for yourself, you won't worry about betrayal as much. When you can imagine a beautiful life even in the absence of romantic love, finding love or losing it again won't seem nearly as scary.

This doesn't mean you have to give up on ever finding love. But right now, finding the right man is just too important to you. I understand that, and I can relate to it very well. But you have to work your way past that. You have to forget men for a while and think only of yourself and your son. He is about to be a big kid, sooner than you can imagine. Slow down and drink him in. Drink yourself in, too. Drink in your life as it is, right now. Recognize how much happiness is already at your fingertips, and savor it as much as you can.

As Arthur Ashe once said, "Start where you are. Use what you have. Do what you can." There is no injustice in your life, not anymore. You are healthy and your son is healthy, and this world wants nothing but happiness for both of you. I know it's not that easy. But just for today, pretend that it is. Love yourself and love him. Maybe this is exactly where you're supposed to be.

Polly

Why Don't the Men I Date Ever Love Me?

Dear Polly,

This weekend, after eighteen months together, my boyfriend told me that he cared very deeply for me and that we had the best partnership he'd ever experienced but he did not love me, because there was a spark missing.

So he ended things in a kind and mature way. We're both in our thirties, and the entire thing has been kind and mature and caring (and sexy and vulnerable and honest) from the beginning. I've dated my share of guys who were bad partners, and this guy was a good one.

And although I am hurt, I get it. I also know that he was always a little bit on the fence about letting me fully into his life. (Literally and metaphorically: Whenever I would go to his apartment, there would never be a place for me to sit. He would have clothes and books and projects piled on every single one of his chairs and his sofa.)

So I kept waiting for him to start taking the actions that would let me in, and he kept waiting for the spark that would make him want to move forward. And in the meanwhile, we made a fun little team.

In the end, although I am sad that he and I aren't going to continue our team, I respect him and I get it. And to be honest, at my core I'm feeling a bit of relief. I want someone who wants to let me in fully.

What is flooring me is the piece about how he didn't love me. None of the guys I've dated long-term have ever loved me. They've liked me a gosh-darn awful lot, but boy-oh-boy do they not want to pull out those three little words.

And I think I'm lovable. Both in my innate humanness and in my adult life. I have my shit together. I went to a therapist as a preemptive measure because I knew this most recent boyfriend and I were about to have either the breakup conversation or the "let's start taking steps toward building a life together" conversation, and I wanted to talk through how to approach both scenarios.

My therapist said, "There's nothing about you that is getting in your own way. You have remarkable communication and emotional coping skills, and you and your boyfriend have a highly evolved partnership." She used the words "highly evolved." She did warn me that the fact that he wasn't physically making space for me in his apartment was a red flag, which, you know, I knew. We agreed that whatever happened between me and the boyfriend would happen in a mature and respectful way and that I would be able to handle it vis-à-vis my remarkable coping skills, and all of these things have come true and I'm still not fucking lovable? I should be *cherished*.

I realize this sounds like a female version of the typical nice guy who wonders why no girls like him but never wants to make a move. I'd like to think that there's a difference between "I'm a good person, why won't you date me?" and "I'm a good partner, why don't you love me?" but maybe there isn't. I also know that the big difference between me and the typical nice guy is when I got broken up with, I didn't go, "Whyyyyyyyyyy?" I went, "Okay, that's sad, but it's true and right and reasonable." (That typical nice guy doesn't know what the truth of a relationship is, and I know what the truth of a relationship is. But I ache that the truth is always "I don't love you, good-bye," instead of "I love you, but good-bye.")

I know I am not owed love. I also wonder sometimes if I don't know what love actually feels like, because so many grown men have told me it's been missing from our relationships. (One came back a year later and said, "Oh, wow, I did not realize that I loved you when we dated, I am so sorry.")

So, dear Polly, what is love? Why is it missing from my highly evolved partnerships?

Sparkless

—m—

Dear Sparkless,

I have two things to tell you. First, this guy was going to dump you no matter what. He says he never had enough of a spark for you. Sometimes men imagine that they're going to be blown away by someone, literally knocked off their feet by a babe straight out of a Doritos commercial. But other times, men just don't find your personality intriguing enough. They might like YOU—being around you, going out to dinner with you, sleeping with you, having brunch with you the next day. But they don't necessarily find themselves fully engaged and interested in who you really are. They don't want to sit and talk unless there are a few cold beers and some snacks nearby. They don't want to walk and talk unless the two of you are on the way to a movie.

I was always paranoid about this when I was younger, because there was always so much evidence that the guy du jour liked being part of a "fun little team" and getting laid regularly and spending time with a talkative, funny woman, but *he didn't necessarily love me.* Even though it made me feel paranoid, I found evidence of this in little things: He wanted to catch a movie instead of having dinner together. He wanted to meet up with his friends after one drink at a bar together. He wanted to listen to the radio in the car instead of talking.

But actually, it's a little rare to find someone who loves you so much that he just loves to talk, talk, talk with you for hours. Plenty of dudes will want to form a "fun little team" with you, particularly if you're smart and highly evolved and you have your shit together. Your stock will always be high. There will always be lots of dudes with projects strewn all over their apartments who will take in your easygoing nature and your eighteen-month-long ability to suspend your disbelief and go with the flow indefinitely.

There's nothing wrong with you, in other words. You're probably attracting a wider swath of men than is good for you. They aren't self-selecting themselves out of contention, because you seem perfectly healthy and reasonable. If you seemed impatient or intolerant, you might slough off some of the wishy-washy slackers in the mix. If you were a little temperamental, you might lose all but the most fervent admirers. Instead, you are healthy and sane and no one will object to being a team, and when you hit month eighteen, you'll (very wisely) assess the situation with your therapist: "Welp, he's either going to pop the question or hit the road, and I need to be fully emotionally prepared for either eventuality."

Okay, this is where the record screeches to a stop. You seriously *didn't know* if he was going to say "Let's be together forever" or "I like you bunches, but I never want to see you again"?

I don't get that. It makes me wonder if you're really showing up or not. It makes me wonder if you don't want, so badly, to be someone's dream girl that you've got your hands on all of the sliders and the knobs (sorry!) at all times, controlling all the levels to achieve the perfect mix. Does he look impatient? Turn up the tempo. Does he seem bored? Pump up the bass. Does he seem on edge? Turn down the treble. Play up the mid-range.

You write, "I know what the truth of a relationship is." Sometimes when someone writes something that straightforward, it's the least true thing in the entire letter. If you knew the truth of this relationship, wouldn't you know whether you'd be together for another day or another four decades? Wouldn't I know a thing or two about you or about him? I get that you can't put too many details in your letter or you might be recognized. But I can't tell from your letter whether you were madly in love with this guy. I don't know if he deserved that love or not. I don't know what all of these other wishy-washy exes were like.

Your letter is all about you. You're really asking me if you're capable of being passionately loved or not. But you haven't told me anything *about* you. You haven't mentioned any details or any troubles in your past relationships or any overarching flaws you might have or repeated mistakes you might have made. In fact, the most detailed bit of your letter is the part where your therapist assures you—before she knows if you'll be getting dumped or getting engaged—that you're 100 percent healthy and evolved and approved for future marriage or future singledom. Either way, you are a government-certified, grade-A, consumer-friendly woman, approved for multiple uses, from forming a fun little team to kind, healthy, mature fence-sitting!

Your real problem is that you're *sure* you have a problem. Because you're pretty sure that you have a problem, you're hiding. You're putting up with whatever. You're never getting ruffled or hurt. When someone breaks up with you, you're not yelling, "Whyyyyy?!!!" In fact, you imply that only a weak or less evolved person would do that. You imply that you aren't a weak person, you're not crazy, you're not fucked-up, you're evolved, you're healthy, you have proof: Your therapist will vouch for you. You have "remarkable communication and emotional coping skills."

You're so good at being GOOD. But how good are you at being YOU? You know what makes a spark? A real human being with a bad attitude who's tired of moving shit just to sit down in a motherfucker's apartment. A woman who, after eighteen months of doing everything together, doesn't sigh and say, "Okay. I'm hurt, but I totally get it." She says, "HOLY FUCK, I THOUGHT YOU WERE ABOUT TO POP THE FUCKING QUESTION. THIS IS SUCH A FUCKING CURVEBALL. [*Knocks a pile of books off a chair to sit down.*] I just wish I hadn't worn these fucking tall shoes, they're killing me, and I thought I should wear them in case we needed to go out somewhere nice to celebrate! [*Takes off shoes and throws them at the wall.*] GODDAMN IT! FUCK THIS!!!! [*Grabs a sketch from some pile of shitty sketches and rips it into a million pieces. Throws body onto filthy carpet and sobs, noting bits of filth in carpet while sobbing.*]"

Okay, so that was a dramatization of some messy behavior. I'm not trying to tell you to be more of a psycho and someone will love you completely. But you *do* need to be *something*. Are you afraid of being something?

Because let me tell you the god's honest truth: A lot of women out there are afraid of being something. The template for us is pretty clear: We are meant to have clean skin, a pleasant demeanor, and a nice rack. I'm not speaking up against nice racks, Lord knows. But there are lots of ladies around me, everywhere I go, who hesitate to say what they're thinking and feeling. They go with the flow; they never make waves. And eventually, they don't even seem to know what makes them who they are. They live to serve. They read the books that other people are reading. They say the pleasant things that other people are saying. They never put their needs first, unless it indirectly serves someone else—a manicure, some highlights. They make sure everyone around them is 100 percent satisfied. Like grocery store managers. Like customer service reps. Like masseuses who also give free happy endings.

If that sounds sexist or demeaning, then it's by design. The developed world is packed to the gills with shiny, pretty sheep who will never step on your toes. I know many representatives of the middle-class suburban version of this, and I even know women in creative fields who pull the same "Me, too!" face in everything they do. It's soul sucking and it's problematic and let me just say, too, that it is a fucking snooze.

When someone says to me, "I try to be nice," or "We make a good team," or "I like for things to be clean," or "I'm pretty organized," you know what I think? Well, first I think, "I need to be nicer and clean my fucking house a little better." But then I think, "Jesus. Why don't you try being a dick and striking out on your own and making a fucking mess for a change?" And also I can see it in some of these husbands' eyes. This woman is holding it down at home, and god forbid she do anything else.

I know I'm digressing, Sparkless. But you *do* have a spark. If you wanted to be swept up by some conformist everyman who replaced the multiple projects with a clean condo and a straight job, you could do that quite easily. There's a more average bear that will love, love, love this highly evolved, communicative self you present to the world.

I think you want a project-obsessed boyfriend because *you* want to have projects of your own. You aren't writing to me so that I'll tell you that some man will love you someday. You aren't writing to me to prove that you're healthy enough and now you're ready to be cherished. You're writing to me because you're ready to cherish yourself.

Like you yourself wrote, *YOU SHOULD BE CHERISHED.*

I want you to get out some colorful markers, and I want you to write these words fifty times, on the same page: "You SHOULD BE cherished. You should be *cherished*. You. Should. Be. Cherished."

You don't cherish yourself. You do whatever what's-his-face wants to do, for the sake of the fun little team, for the sake of demonstrating your good communication skills. Just admit it. You never draw lines in the sand. He says, "We need to talk, it's serious." And you don't say, "WHAT do you MEAN motherfucking WHAT?!! TELL ME RIGHT NOW." You say, "Okay," and then make an emergency trip to your therapist and discuss all of the possibilities, and then you show up the next day, well rested and prepared to discuss either ending it or nailing it down. That sounds perfectly sane and wonderful, but that's not fair to you. You are cherishing him, and cherishing your therapist, and cherishing sanity, and cherishing evolved-lady living, but you aren't cherishing *you.*

Don't you deserve something beyond falling right in line with the other perfect, shiny ladies who deserve doting husbands? Don't you deserve a bigger, brighter existence than the ones they might be perfectly satisfied with?

You aren't satisfied with "evolved." That's not enough for you. If it were, you'd be more sure of your spark, and remarks about lacking a spark wouldn't get under your skin. You wouldn't take some dude's ambivalence personally.

And look, you'd also feel more alive and less worried if you felt comfortable with simply being good. Because even the ladies who step right in line and aim to please, they have lots of spark, if that's what makes them happy. You want more than that. The lack of spark within you comes from the conflict between WHO YOU TRY TO BE and WHAT YOU REALLY WANT FOR YOURSELF. You want more. You act like you don't want more, you act like you're satisfied, but in fact you want a lot more.

I don't know what, specifically, you want. Maybe you want the freedom to say exactly what you mean, instead of saying the "right" thing. Maybe you want to be assertive and bossy, but you don't like women who do that, so you're afraid. Maybe you want to be the one with the projects strewn all over the place.

I used to date men who were obsessed with their creative projects. After a while, I realized that I didn't want them. I wanted to *be* them. I thought being close to that energy might be enough. I thought that being loved by someone who was willing to give himself completely to the creative process was enough. I met a musician once who was consumed by his creations. I put him on a pedestal. I had so much crazy lust for him it was almost stupid. But it wasn't him—I hardly knew him—it was his focus, his total involvement and belief in what he did, that made me crazy. I wanted to have that kind of passion for myself. I should've been cherished. I refused to cherish myself. It was easier to pretend that all of that magic and passion belonged to someone else and that I had to ask permission to get a little taste of it.

You should be cherished, too. Cherish yourself. What kind of work are you doing in therapy? Is it time to stop being so good and start discovering what's going to transform your life into something big and vibrant and shocking? Do you want to get little pats on the head and control your expectations and quietly hope for more? Or do you want to say, once and for all, "NO MORE KIND, MATURE SLEEPWALKING. NO MORE WISHY-WASHY DUDES WHO LOVE THEMSELVES BUT FIND ME WANTING."

It's time to forget about being lovable. And in fact, it's time to forsake someone else's idea of what gives you a spark or no spark. Block the "other" from this picture. No more audience. You are the cherished and the cherisher. You are the eminently lovable and the lover. You are a million brilliant sparks, flashing against a midnight sky. Stop making room for someone else to sit down. Fuck "good" partners. Fuck waiting to be let in. You are already in. You are in. Cherish yourself.

Fuck wondering if you're lovable. Fuck asking someone else, "Am I there yet?" Fuck listening for the answer. Fuck waiting, alone, for a verdict that never comes. Don't grow up to be one of those women with a perpetual question mark etched into her brow: *Am I good? Am I lovable? Am I enough?*

You are here. Sit down. Feel your potential in this moment. You have accepted too little for too long. That is changing today. Breathe in. Draw a picture of yourself. Tape it to the wall, with the words "YOU ARE HERE." You are here. Cherish yourself.

Polly

V

Identity and Becoming an Artist (Whether You Make Art or Not)

Land of the Lost Artist

Hi, Polly,

I'm a very sensitive person. I have been for as long as I can remember. This sensitivity has brought many positive things into my life, including art. Art has been my #1 ever since some very tough years in high school, when I can remember telling my best friend, "If I only had a camera, that is all that I'll ever need."

I am now twenty-nine. I did everything in my power to release myself from the very average, very midsized, very midwestern city that offered little relief to my restless appetite for cultural activity. I packed all of my things and moved to the West Coast. I lived in five cities across the country and traveled abroad, had several semi-long-term relationships, and earned a master's degree in art. But I still feel very much like the same little seven-year-old girl who asked her big sister to check her books out for her at the library so that she wouldn't have to speak to the librarian. There were always people who would protect me from these fearful situations, but as I got older, I became capable of functioning very well within the social environment that once brought me so much stress.

I just got out of a relationship with a great guy who I thought was "the one," despite the fact that I broke up with him several times, citing my own mental health as the factor when my "higher self" (as the self-help book says) must have known that love should not be so cruel. The truth is, I probably spent a year clinging on to him for safety. He was the one person in my life at that time who truly knew me, who held on to my love with such care. I was never afraid that he would hurt me. And yet I treated him so poorly. He won't take me back now. It's taken a while for me to drag myself out of my comfortable position in his arms.

I am now living with my parents in the midwestern city that I once loathed, trying to convince myself that "it's not so bad" and "you could really DO some THINGS here! Why not?" But in the back of my mind, I am anxiously awaiting my future life as a failed artist in a boring city. The hard part is knowing that I could leave, go somewhere alone, and figure it out there. I've done it many times over. But am I just escaping? Is this what I have been doing all along? Am I going for someone else's idea of success?

When does a personality trait become a corporate body with rights? Sometimes I feel as if I have to stick up for my art and my personality, because it has brought so much happiness and excitement and challenge into my life. At other times, I feel cursed by my own genetic disposition. Like an insect that circles the same lightbulb over and over again, always trying to satisfy its craving for brightness, when the brightest thing is always just outside of its reach, a place that is closer to where it originally came from.

I could say that I am trying hard to accept myself fully, to embrace the here and now in whatever shape that takes without relinquishing my decisions to the opinions of others, but I also just want to say that it is terribly lonely to feel like I am forever stuck in some kind of waiting room, the kind with interesting magazines and stylish furniture, while everyone else seems to move in and out with such dedication and consequence.

Where do I go from here?

Lost Artist

—⟋⟍—

Dear Lost Artist,

Other people will always appear to move with dedication and consequence. How else does a person behave when people are watching? We all pretend that our decisions and accomplishments took us in a straight line forward, decisively moving from one success to the next. We gloss over that year wasted looking at old photos or washing our hardwood floors over and over, wishing that we'd create something of consequence instead. We don't mention the year we started and stopped three different screenplays or furiously typed out bad poetry at our go-nowhere temp jobs.

I used to write bad poems from my lonely desk in a bank office at the top of a downtown San Francisco skyscraper. I was living with my boyfriend from college, but he was working nights as a bartender, partially to avoid the clingy psycho chick he had rather unwisely agreed to shack up with. I rarely saw him. I had no friends in town. My boyfriend's friends were not really my friends, which somehow I didn't figure out until we graduated and moved across the country together. But even *they* didn't seem sure if they were friends with each other at the time. One of them would complain to me that another one was going to inherit his father's business and effortlessly become rich, which made him very envious. When I tried to talk to another one about how bad my relationship was, she'd say, "Shut up, that's silly. You're thinking too much. You shouldn't be so insecure." So that was that.

Let the record show that I wasn't exactly stellar friend material myself. I mean, I was a clingy psycho chick who wrote bad poetry at work all day. But somehow, those poems felt like thin threads connecting me to something real and true somewhere inside me that wasn't easy to access. Somehow, even though

I knew my poems weren't very good, I felt reassured by them. My loneliness took some pretty clichéd shapes: A Halloween pumpkin I threw out the window of our second-story apartment. A sea of faceless workers, moving with dedication and consequence, while I floated along, forlorn and self-conscious, worried and scared and skinless. I was lost and I needed to admit it. I needed to record the fact that there was always lint on my tights. I needed to remember that my dumb suit shrank in the rain. I needed to remember that my skin was breaking out horribly, and when I went to a new dermatologist and he learned that I had a boyfriend, he told me, "We are going to make you kissable for the holidays."

Today, this comment would make me laugh out loud. But back then, I felt like I was living on some strange planet inhabited by heartless, careless aliens who for some reason wanted to grab me by the back of the head and smash my face into the carpet until I cried uncle. My boyfriend, with whom I was supposed to live happily ever after, recoiled at the sight of me. He was working in a bar filled with hot girls, and I was an angry neurotic with bad skin. I was paralyzed. He didn't want me to talk anymore. There had to be somewhere else to put everything inside me.

This is how it begins. This is when a personality trait becomes a corporate body with rights. You simply resolve to believe in your experience, to make something out of those feelings. You simply decide that the world doesn't fit you quite right, it's not that comfortable, and it never will be. And yes, let's admit that other people sometimes *do* move with more dedication and consequence, especially compared with those of us who are slowed down by this need to write it down, to turn it into something real. Other people can focus on the bottom line, which is uplifting and uncomplicated. Other people can simply trill, *"Great, I'll be kissable for the holidays!"*

But because these people have it a little easier than us,

because they're not moving through molasses every few days, because they don't overthink things or feel crazy emotions they never intended to feel, because they can keep the world at arm's length and suspend their disbelief and run with the pack and be team players and all of the other stuff that our dim-witted, reductive culture demands, WE GET TO CALL OURSELVES ARTISTS.

I used to hate the word "artist" and hate anyone who had the supreme gall to call herself one. I also hated it when people called themselves writers. I didn't care if they got paid or not. It was pretentious.

I like calling myself an artist now for the same reasons I hated it before. Being an artist means taking up a little extra space without apology. It means allowing yourself to annoy other people with your deluded views of yourself. It means rubbing people the wrong way by acting like your experiences add up to something more. No one is supposed to believe such a narcissistic thing, of course. If your experiences add up, it better be all about god or public service or making a bankroll. It better not be personal or messy or vague or emotional, with no fucking dollar signs attached. Don't you know that people are starving and dying? Who the FUCK are you?

An artist's answer to that question is, "Well, who the fuck are YOU, exactly?" Artists are not easy people to like. Their feelings often come before yours. That's how they have to live sometimes, just to remember, just to locate the center of the thing. They rarely make themselves kissable for the holidays.

It sounds selfish, I know. Some of us have no choice but to give ourselves *a lot* of space. When things get blurry and people are unkind to us, we have to stop and dwell in that blurry space. We have to experience the full brunt of an insult—we have to swallow the bitterest pill, the sharpest words, ingest and metabolize these things until we're weak and wan—in order to be strong. We have to welcome our clingiest, ugliest monster self into the room and love that sad, ugly monster dearly in order to one day be beautiful and generous and resilient. Yes, it sounds selfish, but it's also a route to being less selfish. Trust that.

You might look back someday and draw a straight line from world travel to the West Coast back to the Midwest, selecting out the victories and skimming over the flailing and the second-guessing. But recognize, today, that this skidding, stuttering, stalling point is one of the victories, too. This is your time of reckoning. Of course you'll need a practical route out of your parents' house. The Midwest feels oppressive to you because of the way you're living right now. Of course there are artists there! But you struggle with the sense that where you are is small and average and you will always be a misfit there. You should work hard to either deconstruct your ideas about the place or explore new places instead.

That doesn't mean you won't be a misfit everywhere. Artists are always misfits. Even when you plant them in artist colonies, they feel like the misfits among other misfits. That misfit energy is good. But if you throw in all of the signs and signifiers of powerlessness from your childhood—and that's what's in the mix when you live in your parents' home, whether you have a good attitude about it or not—you're really giving yourself too steep a hill to climb. You need to live on your own again. Decide where you want to live. Make it happen. You don't have to believe in this decision every single day. You just have to earn a little money and save a little money and then pack your stuff and arbitrarily move somewhere.

There is the artist, and then there's this pragmatic person within you who bails you out when you're drowning. Don't let the artist fuck with what the pragmatist is trying to do. But *do* let the artist take up a lot of space. Let the artist call herself an artist, even to her parents' skeptical friends. Practice saying it out loud to exactly the people who are the most likely to think you're a fucking joke.

You're an artist if you create art, period. You're a writer if you write. First, you have to claim the title. You can't work hard until you claim the right. (For women, I think, that's particularly true.)

Artists, pretentious or not, blustery and swaggery or self-abnegating, need to find their faith in their work all over again, every morning of their lives. You need to devote yourself to your religion, Lost Artist. You need to cling to it the way you once clung to your ex-boyfriend.

It makes sense that you're not there yet, at age twenty-nine, in your parents' house. You want other things besides your art. But don't even think about throwing your art aside. Don't think for a second that it's a liability, a personality flaw, just an extra thing that you need, that slows you down, that regular people don't need.

In fact, stop thinking about regular people. They will never matter as much as you think they do when you're twenty-nine years old. You *will* move with dedication and consequence. Believe it. This is your era of reckoning. Write that on the wall of your childhood bedroom in big letters. Writing on the wall is precisely the sort of obnoxious shit that a real artist would do. This way station, this troubling pause, this return to nowhere land, is *also* a victory.

When I finally quit my temp job at the bank downtown, the new temp I'd trained, who hated me for some reason—maybe because the job sucked and I was much younger than him—called me and asked me, "What are all these documents you left on your laptop?"

"Those are poems," I said. "You can throw them out."

"They're pretty disturbing. One starts out, 'I threw out the pumpkin . . .'"

"Yes, that's one of my poems. You can delete it."

"Another one says, 'Sad and small, hoping for something to save me . . .'"

"You can delete *all* of them," I said. "Just delete them."

What I should've said was, "Why the fuck do *you* care?" I can't imagine someone talking to me that way these days. It makes me sad, the way some people talk to young people, knowing they're embarrassed and vulnerable.

Maybe I'm less likable now than I was then. Maybe in the intervening years, I've willed my personality flaws into a corporate body with rights. I don't have to mumble an apology and feel ashamed of myself. I know that I deserve to take up space. I still have copies of those poems somewhere. Even if I didn't, I could still remember them. That was the year I realized I was a bright, burning light, and no fucking insect was going to persuade me to hate myself for it.

Let's fly into *your* future and look back at this year in your history in our minds. This was the year that you really *knew* that you were an artist, first and foremost. This was the year you committed to what came next.

Remember this year? It was a good year, actually. This was the year you stopped waiting around for things to happen. And somehow, as soon as you stopped waiting, as soon as you started doing things, making things, claiming your own space, speaking up for yourself? That's when your real life began.

Polly

Lame Job, Lame Life

Dear Polly,

I'm single for the first time in nearly ten years. Since being dumped last summer, I've spent a good amount of time looking at my life more closely, and I do not like what I see.

I work at a small company in Los Angeles. When I started there I was twenty-three, just graduating from college, and had decided that I was going to try my hand at becoming a freelance writer and comedian. This job was supposed to be one that helped pay the bills without draining me mentally and emotionally. I wanted to make my living by making people laugh and creating things with other people who loved to do that, too. I told myself that I'd take one year to hone my craft, save in the meantime, and then go out on my own to be the successful person I was destined to be.

Here I am four years later, still with the same company. I make myself the same promise every year, and every year I've let it fall to the wayside. I've somehow ended up in a leadership position, but it's unfulfilling and I do absolutely nothing creative. I love my co-workers and the company, but I really couldn't give a shit. I'm worried that this will eventually become obvious to people. The little fulfillment I get from my job comes from these amazing people I work with, who are all infinitely more capable and intelligent and creative than I could ever pretend to be.

I think I know how I got here, and the answer embarrasses

me. Since I can remember, my life has been about boys. I started dating at fourteen and now recognize that my self-worth was (is?) deeply tied to how men feel about me. Everything else—my career, where I lived, the college I went to—was decided based on some combination of convenience and "the next logical step." I've sort of floated through my life following these men down their paths, while every once in a while feeling worthless enough to make blind, halfhearted attempts at finding my own. Since realizing this, I've tirelessly analyzed how it has affected my life, and it bums me out more and more and more.

My most recent relationship was nearly six years in length. While we were together, I dabbled in comedy and a few people encouraged me, but I never seriously pursued it. I was more concerned with making this man—who I knew didn't really love me—love me, and I regret it so, so much. If I had a chance to talk to myself back then, I'd warn her against relationships, period. I'd try to shake sense into her until her head came off.

What's sad is that my relationship with my job is the same as my relationship was with my ex: I'm exhausted, I constantly feel undervalued, and if I'm being completely honest, I'm giving about 30 percent across the board. I am certain that something out there is a better fit and I have an idea of what it looks like, but I'm certain that I'm wholly undeserving and unprepared for it.

I never got in the habit of hard work or pouring my energy into my passions because I was too busy trying not to be alone. I'm trying now, but I'm twenty-seven, and at this point it just feels hopeless. Even if I thought I was good enough to pursue my dream, I've got no body of work. No experience. No training. Just a hunch that I might be funny and the idea that it's what I'd rather be doing.

Maybe I'm not funny, maybe I'm not a creative person, and maybe I should just be grateful for this comfortable, "fun" job that someone else would love and that I'm hardly qualified for.

How do I give myself the courage, or the motivation, to try and prove myself wrong?

Sincerely,
Stuck Phoning It In

———∿∿———

Dear SPII,

The words "I'm twenty-seven, and at this point it just feels hopeless" just make me laugh and laugh, the deep, smug chuckle of a nasty old crone with a superior attitude. Listen up, dummy: You spent four years at a mediocre job. *That is the best possible start for a creative career.* It's actually much more dangerous to never have done a single thing to support yourself and *then* discover that your giant creative ambitions are not going to usher you straight to the widely adored, shiny princess life of your dreams. I live in L.A. I know people who've been chasing their creative dreams with less and less vigor for TWENTY YEARS now. Having had a concrete professional existence is great and very typical of many (if not MOST) successful funny-person trajectories. You will look back at this job and say, "I'm glad I did that. It taught me all about the life I *didn't* want. It helped me to never look back."

I myself began my writing career as a highly celebrated assistant executive secretary at a bank. Then I moved into desktop publishing (see also typing). All the while I wondered if maybe my creativity and my writing talent were both just self-protective ego illusions. Thanks to the dot-com boom, I got to start my real writing career at the tender age of twenty-five, which then seemed to me a little late in the game but now looks absurdly lucky. But then the tech bubble burst, and I had to start over. Writers have to start over every few years, honestly. And let's not mince words, that aspect of the creative/writerly path is an UNMITIGATED FUCKING NIGHTMARE.

And there are many low points in the trajectory to (limited) fame and (limited) fortune. Many, many low points. The great irony of being a creative, sensitive, talented love seeker is that you're not always that well suited for such low points. Your brain likes to eat itself alive in a vacuum. You feel needy and unworthy. Having an office job of some sort is not the worst-case scenario for such a person. Even as you half-ass your way through day after day, at least you're not facedown on the carpet at home, feeling lonely and worthless and delusional.

That said, you've reached a point where you cannot sally forth with your current career. The work means nothing to you. You like the place and the people, but you don't like your actual job. You really don't have a choice now. You know you have to pursue your dream at this point. It's not *remotely* too late! It could take you four more years to whip your creative act into shape, and it *still* wouldn't be too late! If you were forty-eight and had kids and were broke, I might tell you to keep your job until you find a new one. But you aren't. In fact, this could be the ideal time to move forward. A second earlier would've been too soon (you would've dropped every project to make your boyfriend love you more, anyway); a second later might be too late (you might've moved into an expensive place or had a kid or had other responsibilities that precluded taking this kind of risk).

This is your moment. Seize your moment, goddamn it! Do not ask about where the courage and motivation will come from. This crisis will *give* you the courage and the motivation you need. It's already there. You're unhappy and you feel like a failure. PERFECT! Use that sad/angry/disappointed energy. Channel it into what you know, deep down in your heart, you love.

Spend the next six months in a state of total obsession. Get up two hours earlier than usual and write before you go to work. Come home and exercise (not optional, sorry), then write for another hour. Read or watch the kind of comedy you love before bed. Don't waste all your time socializing. Do a little socializing on weekends, but focus. Focus! Save your money. Research part-time work you could do for your company; use your slackness as a way to sell a new position where your boss would get your best from you every hour that you're there. Pitch it as win-win. Or pitch working from home half the time to cure your blahs and jack up your productivity. Then overproduce at work, but fit all of your work into a part-time schedule, and fill your prime working hours with writing/comedy. Almost any capable human with a not-that-taxing job can pull this off if they put their mind to it. If you're a manager, investigate other roles or sell your boss on the fact that you're managing via e-mail most of the time anyway.

Of course you will still question what you're doing every stupid day, maybe for the next two decades. Even after you write a hundred funny things, you'll believe that you're all tapped out. I'm always convinced that every essay I write will be my last. I'm always wrong. And I can tell you from experience that if you get up early, drink your caffeine, and fill yourself with the sense that you are going to TURN THIS MOTHER OUT SOMEHOW, SOMEWAY, you will find the inspiration and the tenacity you're looking for. You have to put all the pieces into place, and then you have to let it come to you. It will. Trust!

You will *still* feel like a self-deluded loser most of the time. That's okay. That's the writer's life for you. Take some classes at one of those improv factories, meet some other writers and comedians, discuss your ideas with the creative people at work who probably have side projects of their own. Start owning this goal and living it.

And stop saying shit like "I'm not as creative or as talented as these other people. I don't deserve this, I'm lame compared to them." Stop it. With writing, with comedy, with everything, you're about as talented as you think you are most of the time. People are so delusional about talent, as if you're either pure magic or made of nothing. You know which people think that way? Talentless people. Those who strive, who create, who try, who work hard? They know that about 50 percent of talent comes from working your ass off and the other 50 percent comes from cultivating an extreme arrogance around your particular flavors of genius.

As long as you're walking around saying you don't have it, then you don't. And having it is sometimes as easy as saying, "DAMN I'M GOOD," over and over again. You say it before you start writing. You say it the second you write something decent. You say it when you're done. Can you do that or can't you?

Because I don't think you were made to follow men around, to wait for their cues, and to cower in the presence of creative people. I think you're doing these things out of habit. You think it's audacious to stand up for your talents, to boldly proclaim yourself a writer and take the life that you want and tell the life you don't want to fuck off. Listen, it doesn't matter if every human on the planet would kill for your job. If you don't want it, then to hell with it.

Stop being grateful for scraps. Everything good in my life has surged forth from one crucial moment or another when I said, "I am not settling for these scraps anymore. I want more than this for myself."

In my seventh year as a staff TV critic, I kept saying to my husband, "So many people would kill for this job." I felt spoiled. But I didn't want to write about TV anymore. I was done. I knew that freelance writing was going to be a total crapshoot, and I had two small kids and a big mortgage to worry about. But it was time to move on. I needed to try something new.

I tried and I failed a lot, and this was after fifteen years of professional writing. I went through a long stage where I couldn't get my editor to reply to a pitch anymore, so I just sat around freaking out all day long. You will have times like that, too. But don't torment yourself by lamenting over the big picture of your career every goddamn day. Make concrete goals and meet them and power forward. When you can't move forward with your work, go on a run or read a book, then try again afterward.

Above all, believe. Cultivate your swagger. Make this your new religion: You are funny and talented, and you're going to try something new. This is the exact right time for that. This is the most important year of your life, and for once you are NOT going to let yourself down. If you fall down and feel depressed, you will get back up. If you feel lethargic and scared, you will try something else: a new routine, a new roommate situation, a healthier diet. You will read books about comedy. You will work tirelessly and take pride in your tireless work. And you will take time every few hours to stop and say to yourself, "Look at me. I'm doing it. I'm chasing my dream. I am following my calling." It doesn't matter if your dreams come true, if agents swoon and audiences cheer. Trust me on that: It truly doesn't matter. What matters is the feeling that you're doing it, every day. What matters is the work—diving in, feeling your way in the dark, finding the words, trusting yourself, embracing your weird voice, celebrating your quirks on the page, believing in all of it. What matters is the feeling that you're not following someone else around, that you're not half-assing this, that you're not waiting for something to happen, that you're not waiting for your whole life to start.

What matters is you, all alone at your desk at five in the morning. I write this from my own desk at five in the morning, my favorite place, a place where I know who I am and what I'm meant to accomplish in this life. Savor that precious space. That space will feel like purgatory at first, because you'll realize that it all depends on you. That space will feel like salvation eventually, because you'll realize that it all depends on you.

Polly
P.S. DAMN I'M GOOD.

Do I Make Music or Have a Family?

Dear Polly,

I'm a highly accomplished jazz pianist, but I also write pop and techno and musical theater. I have a lot of facets to my art, so it takes a lot of time, and it also makes it harder to earn a living, since I'm competing with people who are more specialized. But I have so much to express I feel like I have to do it all. On top of that, I'm interested in music and the brain and would like to go to graduate school.

I've been living in New York for seven years, writing music and performing and also making ends meet as a private piano teacher, church pianist, etc. I don't have many friends here, and I have been feeling increasingly isolated.

Five years ago, I met a girl, we clicked, and pretty soon we were living together. We had a loving, supportive relationship, but there were also some boundaries. I needed a lot of space to do my music, and I also had a lot of trepidation about the future, which got in the way of my work.

I knew that she wanted to eventually get married and have kids, so I tried as hard as I could to succeed before then. I also knew she wanted to move back to San Francisco (where we're both from) so she could raise kids near her parents. I gave up most of my twenties trying to get some kind of success, and now I'm thirty-two and haven't succeeded.

Last year, somewhat unexpectedly, she got a job in San

Francisco. I didn't want to stand in the way of her career, and we're both pretty easygoing, so we figured that we'd figure it out. About six months ago, she told me that she needed a firm commitment to our relationship and raising a family, or else she needed to leave the relationship. I couldn't give her one. I love San Francisco, but the music scene, and the possibility of making a worldwide splash, is pretty small. Part of me wants to move back there and start a family, but I also feel like it might be the end of my dreams. Maybe I'm deluded, but doing my art, and the possibility that maybe one day it will connect with a lot of people, makes me happy and gives me a sense of purpose and identity.

I've talked with a lot of people with children, and I can't see how I could make it work. The older musicians I've met who've started families seem pretty disappointed in general, and I can't say that their families seem to be a very effective consolation prize. I'm sure that I love her, but I don't know if I can attain my potential and live my destiny with her.

I feel like I am choosing between a life of crushing, monastic loneliness in New York or a life of frustrated compromise in San Francisco. I have a genuine gift, and I simply must put it to good use. I can't give up on my dreams, but I don't think I'll ever find another girl like her. It's not too late to get her back, but soon it will be. I think the essential question is whether I would be happier as an unattached, free artist or as a married dad who is also an artist. I think my girlfriend (should we get back together) would be okay with it if I pursued my art, but I wonder also if that isn't entering into a compromise where nobody is really happy. I wonder if I'm too black-and-white in my thinking or if the strength to resist temptation and compromise is what makes a truly great artist or person.

I guess it comes down to this: What's it all about? Is it about happiness? What is greater, the happiness of hearing your orchestral work performed by the London Phil or playing with your kid on a rainy day? The happiness that some strangers get from hearing your song when it's exactly what they needed, or the happiness that your family gets from having you around? Is it knowing you had the courage to go your own way and live an extraordinary life or being enmeshed in a group of people whose happiness is tied in with your own? Is it about giving happiness or getting happiness?

Yours humbly,
Burdened

—⁓—

Dear Burdened,

First of all, I find it troubling that you claim that you haven't succeeded. You're highly accomplished, you work hard, and you pour yourself into your compositions and collaborations every single day. Working on your music gives you a sense of purpose and identity and makes you happy. *That is the very definition of success.* There *is* nothing else. I've been paid and I've been popular and I've connected with people, but every single day I wake up and what I need, more than anything else, is a sense of purpose and identity. I need to write things that make me happy, that make me feel like I'm bringing something worthwhile into the world that wasn't there before. Ego rewards and praise are nice, but you can't carry them with you or ingest them and that positive glow you get from them fades no matter what. You are still just you, a talented artist who wants to create, every day. An artist who wants to work very hard, who wants to exceed yesterday's high-water mark and create something even more entrancing and seductive and glorious.

So stop waiting for the future to arrive. You are here. You are a success. As someone who also writes songs and loves it, I have to say, I picture you collaborating and performing and composing and I think, "My god, that must be so great." What you do is the most enviable thing on the planet, as far as I'm concerned. And you're really doing it! You're committed to it and you believe in it and it brings you joy. Just because the crass world outside tells you what you do is insignificant until you're raking in adoration and cold hard cash doesn't mean it's right. Your existence might feel monastic and money might be tight, but you're just working on your art.

So stop it with the self-defeating talk. Start making victorious sounds, and the world will rush in to greet you with more enthusiasm.

Likewise, it's extremely self-defeating to believe that you have to choose between art and love. I hate it when I hear young people saying they don't want to have kids because they'd have to give up their art or their careers, since we all know now that you can never have it all. Fuck that! Yes, it's hard to balance a career and a family and love. In my experience, though, it's far more difficult to live a solitary artist's existence and come home to an empty apartment every night than it is to juggle the elements that make up a full life.

I understand the romantic notion that saying no to a compromised existence as a husband and father and breadwinner is the only way to be a real artist. I grasp that plenty of world-famous artists, particularly touring musicians, have lived that way. But I firmly believe that you have to go for ALL of the things you want, at once. I don't think you should have to sacrifice love for art, or art for love. It sounds to me like your ex understands perfectly well that the man she wants to spend her life with is someone with huge passions and ambitions and, if she wants you, she'll need to accept that your music career is fundamental to your happiness.

That said, I think marriages work best when both partners, as much as possible, contribute equally. You have to stay committed to supporting yourself, both financially and emotionally. You have to earn money and maintain friendships and keep yourself healthy. When relationships get lopsided—one person works to support the other person's art—things can go south.

But don't tell yourself that true artists always forge ahead alone. Like many other young men who are passionate about their creative pursuits, I think you're unduly fixated on the idea that love will block you from your true desires. A good partner is not like some Teri Garr character, constantly whining, "Come back to bed, baby, and stop thinking about aliens/saving the world/syncopated melody lines!" I think girlfriends who want a firm commitment sometimes end up sounding like scary menaces who will force you to give up on your dreams just to juggle dirty diapers all day long. But trust me, what they really want more than anything else is to have a practical conversation about what a life together, long-term, might look like, and they want to know whether or not you're mature enough and hardworking enough to handle all of it. I'm telling you right now I believe that you are.

I also think it's deceptive to ask older, married musicians with kids about this issue. People who never got enough ego rewards from their art will make the same noises, whether they have kids or not. Kids are largely beside the point. Look closely at the people you're talking to. Are they extremely happy and daring? Are they the sorts of people who composed music at a very young age, like you did, or are they the sorts of people who tended to sell themselves short, toured with this or that show, and then settled down and felt envious of other, more successful musicians? Did they work hard around the clock, like you do, or did they drink and play gigs and hang out around the clock? Were they idealists who believed in love (I think you might be one of these), or did they always have trouble showing their full selves to their partners and eventually came to see their partners as Teri Garr–style enemies?

You can mold a beautiful future for yourself. You need to stop intellectualizing and turning love into a puzzle. You need to stop accepting less than you deserve, artistically and emotionally. You can't settle for the monastic loneliness you describe. You need to open your heart not just to your art but to the world and the people around you. Even if you decide you can't move to San Francisco and you need to leave your ex behind, you have to start connecting to the world around you in a more open way. You're surrounded by some of the most interesting, thoughtful people in the world right now, Burdened! You need more joy in your life RIGHT NOW, no matter where you end up with your ex.

You also need to ask yourself if you love your ex enough to want to be with her no matter what. I can imagine that San Francisco might be a challenge musicwise. I guess I'd ask for some compromise on her part in the short term there, in exchange for a long-term vision of a life together—if that's what you both truly want. If you're sure that you want her in your life, you have to call her and have a big conversation about the future. Would she consider living in New York for five years in the name of your work? What are each of your worries about a life together? What do you each really want? You were easygoing and a little indecisive before. Now you're adults. It's time to revisit this question. If you love this woman and you very much want her back, you're going to need to make that clear. If that sounds extremely difficult, and not just for internal reasons, then maybe you don't love her enough to go down this path with her.

And maybe, Burdened, you don't really want a family. I can't tell you if you do or you don't. All I can tell you is that the great artists I've read about have something in common: balance. They know what combinations of work and play feed them and make them better at what they do. Sure, some are solitary. But all of them give themselves what they need to succeed. They don't work themselves into the ground every day and feel punished and isolated and alone, not usually. Usually, they get up early, go on a walk, do some important thinking, work on their art for four hours straight, eat a nice lunch, work two more hours, read for an hour, go out with friends, and so on. They've refined their routines and have it all down to a science.

What I'm saying is that being an artist takes constant recalibration. As an artist and as an adult, you have to solve new puzzles every day. Successful artists have to keep rebalancing everything in their lives in order to stay inspired and energetic and fully alive. That's true no matter what their circumstances are. And in my experience, being LESS busy doesn't lead to making more/better art. Sometimes it can cause your gears to grind to a halt completely.

Productive artists don't settle for "Oh, I'm in a slump now. I just have to sit here and mope and feel terrible." They look closely at what works at this moment and what doesn't, and they reinvent their schedules every single day.

Above all, you have to dare to reach for everything you want, even when other people say discouraging things. You should dare to reach for ALL OF IT. Going after everything you want makes you a better artist. There is no scarcity of time and money and love in the world.

Your life is happening now. You have to reach for what you love. You're already doing that with your music. Keep doing it, on all fronts. Reach for what you love with abandon, with hope in your heart, with fragility, without knowing exactly what comes next. Reach and never, ever stop reaching.

Polly

This Job Is Killing Me

Dear Polly,

I am a thirty-one-year-old male, and I have a lot of insanely positive things going on in my life. For starters, I am in a wonderful relationship, I have a family that loves me, and I feel healthy and creative.

I have found a small amount of success within an artistic community in Los Angeles. I was always hoping to have a seat at a creative table, and now, I feel, people are really starting to notice my work.

What bothers me is my job. My current job, a temp job that has gone on for too long, is ending, and I am starting to interview for other positions. But I cringe when I go in for interviews because I truly don't want any of the jobs I am applying for. I am not particularly good at working desk jobs. For example, I am sitting here right now, at work, writing this.

I find it difficult to give up so much of my time and hours to a company that doesn't care for me, for a product that has no meaning to me. I come in late, I have difficulty remembering names of businesses and associates we work with, and I feel very lackadaisical about the job. It is difficult for me to get motivated for work I find no value in. But I know that I need a job to afford my life in Los Angeles.

And, as I apply for other jobs, I feel that I cannot even hide my lack of motivation anymore. At thirty-one, I'm feeling a bit too old to be an assistant, but I have no desire to climb any sort of corporate ladder. Truthfully, I keep myself at lower-level positions on purpose, always telling myself, "One day, I'll leave this job. This way I can pursue my art."

So I'm afraid I may have doomed myself to a lifetime of jobs where I will always have one foot out the door. Jobs I cannot commit to, but that I need in order to pay my rent.

I guess my worry is that I am not living up to my potential. I remember a letter you wrote to a lawyer who was having difficulty with her job. You suggested she get in touch with herself to figure out what it was she truly wanted with her life. I read your reply over and over again, and while I'd like to think I have found my artistic calling, as both a performer and a writer, to get to the point where I can be paid for either of those skills feels daunting and near impossible.

And so I go to job interviews and talk about how dedicated and serious I am about administrative work, all while my soul screams at me to drop everything and pursue acting and writing full-time. To give it a shot.

How do I possibly give it a shot when I have bills to pay?

How do I balance what I want with what I need?

Professionally Frustrated, Creatively Fulfilled

—⁂—

Dear PFCF,

Boy, have I been there! Way back in the olden times, when very few people had computers at home and no one had cell phones and, like that line from the Arcade Fire song, we used to wait around for letters to arrive, I had a job as a desktop publisher; that was the glorified term for a typist, in the olden days. And many days, instead of doing my job word processing (another fancy word for typing out the messages that everyone alive does now while they're walking down the street), I'd sit around feeling sorry for myself. Then I would go home to my apartment in San Francisco, and I'd play guitar and sing for five hours at a time.

My roommate at the time was working for a software start-up that she was pretty sure would turn her into a multimillionaire eventually, so she'd come home and I'd be singing in my room and she'd go out for drinks with friends and she'd come home and I'd still be singing and she'd peek into my room and say, "SERIOUSLY, ARE YOU EVER GOING TO LEAVE THIS ROOM?"

She was my friend, but she also thought I was a serious loser. I had no community, no success to speak of. But I loved writing songs. It was my dream.

And like you, I was worried that if I committed to anything more strenuous than a shitty administrative job, I would lose my dream. First some executives at the bank I worked for discovered that I'd gone to what's considered a good school, and they wanted me to join the sales force, coaxing rich people into various investments. *No way.* I quit. Then the technical writer I worked for wanted to promote me. No way. But I did spontaneously start drawing cartoons to illustrate concepts in her training books, and she ended up using them and asking for more.

It was a step in the right direction maybe, but it was only a day job to me. Like you, I figured no day job would ever make me happy. I didn't want to put in the effort to climb the corporate ladder. I didn't want to dress nicely and ride the bus to the financial district. I didn't want to be taken seriously at something I hated.

Eventually, I started saying I wanted to work in graphic design. This was an arbitrary goal, really. I knew how to use all of the page layout software, I could draw reasonably well, so I figured, why not earn more per hour? Thankfully, my roommate caught wind of this and stopped me in my tracks. "Do you even *like* that stuff? Are you even *good* at it? Is that really what you want to do all day, lay out pages? You're a good writer. Why don't you try to get a job at a magazine instead?"

"Writing—whatever," I thought. But I could see her point. Writing was something I didn't hate. I'd taken an extension course in essay writing, and the teacher had told me to quit my job and become a writer. I knew I was good at it, but it always came easily to me, so I discounted its importance.

Eventually, though, in my usual half-assed way, I decided I'd pursue a writing career. I would make writing my day job. How impractical and insane is that? But I happened to know a few magazine editors. I got an internship out of the blue. Then I discovered Suck.com, loved it, and applied for a job there. They hired me, miraculously enough, and I started collaborating with their illustrator on cartoons. Suddenly, just by doing the stuff I'd always been good at, I had an actual career. Not a day job. A career.

To be clear, I'm the kind of person who could've easily stayed in those earlier administrative jobs indefinitely. I was comfortable with underperforming if it meant not having to shower regularly or look people in the eye. But now I have a career where that's possible. I've been working from home since 1998. Eighteen years of skulking around at home smelling bad. I'm living the dream!

The most important thing for me was to avoid a life of punching the clock. The whole idea of being paid to warm a chair and show your face in meetings and add your "yeah, yeah" at the right times—it always chilled me to the bone. And I was terrible at it! It felt oppressive and stupid. I just wanted to be judged for my work, not for my demeanor or my ability to act like a team player. I didn't ever want to be a team player.

I'm not bragging about that. It's not the easiest set of preferences to have, and it made me feel like a loser and a misfit throughout my twenties. But it's hard to pursue success in a world you secretly want to escape.

You're good at collaborating with people, but you're afraid of having your dream overturned by some crappy day job that morphs into a career, with real responsibilities and oppressive time commitments. You're not wrong to fear those things.

That said, don't project "the corporate ladder" onto every job out there. No one is going to make you become a middle manager out of the blue. If you're working for an interesting place, you'll be collaborating with smart, creative people, and that will be engaging and fulfilling in its own way.

When you're doing administrative work, you rarely get looped into the interesting conversations or projects, at least not in any satisfying way. That makes it easy to take a dim view of everything around you. Your salary is low, and it seems like the only way to make more money is to say yes to something you don't want.

If you *are* going to stay in admin jobs, choose your environment carefully. Make sure you're working at a place that's interesting, or at least honorable, run by smart people who have big ideas and energy and care about their work. You need to be around inspired, smart people.

But your letter suggests that it's time for you to move on from your current job. Don't give up on your dream of acting and writing. Find a job that springs from your real skill set. You need to take things you already love doing (whether it's writing or interacting or creating) and then try to think about which jobs and work environments might encourage those things.

You don't have to *adore* the entry-level version of a potential career any more than you like admin work. Nobody likes admin work. You don't even have to be in love with the idea of reaching the top of that field. You just have to be able to look at careers in the field and say to yourself, "Yeah, I could do that without wanting to kill myself every day." It doesn't have to feel like a dream. Magazine writing never seemed like some source of endless glory and inspiration to me; it just seemed like a tolerable, occasionally satisfying way to pay the rent. The good thing about landing in the right career ballpark, though, is that, over the years, you can cut out the less inspiring assignments and focus on the stuff that really excites you.

You will definitely want to speak with people who do the job you're considering. When I was working those admin jobs, I thought about going to law school because being a lawyer seemed respectable and it paid well. Then my dad told me that every lawyer he knew hated his job. So ask around. People will tell you what they love and hate and how satisfied they are. You just have to ask.

I think your day job really needs to be more than a paycheck. You can still pursue your creative dreams, PFCF! You can chase them even as you find other work. It sounds like you're already doing that. Find a job that's related to your dreams, if you can, or that's related to another of your half dreams, and do *that*.

But don't keep underselling yourself and doing work that makes you miserable. It's not healthy to live that way. You have to aim higher and find something that brings you genuine satisfaction. You can't feel like you waste forty hours a week on something arbitrary. You need to make a living, but you don't have to do it by torturing yourself. Taking on more responsibility at something you enjoy will be much easier than engaging in tedious drudgery in the wrong field.

You have to make a commitment to your dreams. Don't let yourself put your dreams second. Don't let the attitudes of the people you work with, now or later, inform you on how "foolish" or "impractical" your dreams are. You have to keep your dreams safe from skeptics. You have to feed them until they grow into something that can't be doubted anymore.

You're already on your way. Take all of your energy and passion and put them into your dream AND your career. You have enough energy and passion for both. And someday, your dream and your career might be one and the same. But even if that never happens? Find a way to enjoy how you spend your waking hours. When you feed your soul and truly savor what you do with your time, that makes it much more likely that your big dreams will come true.

Polly

VI

The Uncertainty Principle

Making Friends (Out of Nothing at All)

Dear Polly,

I'm in my late twenties. I live with a great boyfriend in a great city and have a great job in a field I am passionate about. I have a good relationship with my family and have had many happy connections with all sorts of folks over my lifetime. And yet somehow I find myself at this moment practically friendless.

It's so embarrassing even admitting it. Like I have some kind of disease. I somehow feel the need to defend myself by listing all the friends I've had to show I'm capable of forming friendships and am not a psychopath or a social pariah. But instead I'll list the many reasons why I'm currently in the pickle I'm in.

I moved a lot as a child. Because of this, I had to start over socially every time and didn't grow up alongside my extended family. (When one of my grandparents got sick recently, I even felt awkward calling to wish them well because I knew my aunt, uncle, and cousins were so much more qualified to offer comfort since they live nearby.) Though my reserved nature made this hard on me, I still found tight-knit groups of friends all the way until the end of college. And then, adulthood struck.

Suddenly my friends were dispersed across the entire U.S., and I found myself with nobody to go get a coffee with. And despite many close calls, that's pretty much how it's been for the past five years.

Rationally, I know the answer is to take initiative. But my temperament lends itself to forming friendships like the way water might slowly bubble up from a dry creek bed. Over time and with little fanfare, my connection to a person grows until we are bonded in that mysterious way people bond. Maybe modern life doesn't lend itself to this attachment style. After all, every time, without fail, as soon as something begins to slowly take shape, one of us moves away, and all that potential energy goes "poof."

For a while I coasted (perhaps too much) in the comfort of long-distance calls and Skyping. But my closest friend from college is now deeply involved in restarting her life on the opposite side of the country. And despite all those wonderful things I mentioned at the beginning of this letter, I am so, so, so deeply lonely. To the point where I question everything I ever hoped for from adulthood. If this is really what being an adult means, I don't think I want it anymore. Sure, I can pay my bills, but what I really want is someone to go get Arby's curly fries at 2:00 a.m. with. All my co-workers grew up and went to school and college in the area, meaning they all have extended networks of family and friends built up over a lifetime. God, I want that. I want that friend of the family who's practically a second mother, that uncle who shows up unannounced, that pack of girlfriends you've never celebrated a birthday without.

So in lieu of that lifetime of network building, I'm trying that whole initiative thing in the most pathetic way possible. I made a giant list of ways to make friends. It's an unwieldy beast and includes meet-ups, running groups, classes, exercise groups, Twitter, etc. But against all this desperate trying pushes the grim reality: Making friends is hard work, and everyone is so busy and not interested. Finding people with common ground is suddenly like climbing a mountain, and most of the things I'm interested in seem to attract the retired, recently divorced, or new moms, all of whom are lovely people but who are themselves just looking for other retired, recently divorced, or new-mom types who have things in common with them. And to everyone else I either come on as too desperate or too reserved. Suddenly that thing that used to come so naturally is broken, and trying to fix it is just making things worse. And when I burn out from all the effort, it hits me hard. I stop trying and I just wallow. I'm in one of those spells right now, recuperating and miserable.

I'm not sure if I need advice or reassurance or what. I feel like Quasimodo in the bell tower. But without a hump, what's my excuse?

Friendless

—◊◊—

Dear Friendless,

Someone should really poll women in their late twenties who live in great cities with great boyfriends and have great careers, because I'll bet a lot of them are nearly friendless. This is the downside of living in a gigantic country like the U.S.: You move away for college, you move away for work, you move away because you meet a great guy or girl, and one day you wake up and you're two thousand miles away from anyone who knows you really well. For someone who's not great at small talk, who can never quite hit that lowest common denominator of casual chattiness, who can never quite manage to burble happily about the weather and the news and those cute shoes and the new restaurant down the block, making brand-new friends sounds about as appealing as a trip to the podiatrist. (If you've never been to a podiatrist, please remain in that blissfully ignorant state for as long as you can.)

And if you moved a lot as a kid, you learned to appear satisfied in a crowd, because wandering around asking people to talk to you or play with you is a one-way ticket to the bottom of the social totem pole. "They already have their friends," you told yourself, and fiddled "contentedly" with something in the corner instead. This might be adaptive as a child, but as an adult it just means you're throwing up a protective "I DON'T NEED ANYONE, I'M FINE" face to the world.

So the first thing you have to do is accept that despite appearances you're not all that different from most people your age. The mid- to late twenties are often an apex of friendless desperation. To make matters worse, people feel very self-conscious about their friendlessness at that age, as if everything should've fallen into place a long time ago. Considering how often urban, career-focused Americans move around and turn their lives upside down in their twenties, you'd think most of us would know better.

It's also crucial to remember that even when people "already have their friends" and everything has fallen into place, it can easily fall out of place at any time. Not to mention the many people who look at their existing friendships in their twenties and say, "What the fuck? WHO ARE THESE TERRIBLE PEOPLE?" In fact, my guess is that *most* people your age are in the same boat, even if it doesn't look that way from the outside.

Age twenty-eight was a real low point in my friendship trajectory. I had just moved to L.A. with my boyfriend; we lived down the block from each other. I was living alone for the first time, which was amazing, but I tended to revel in this solitude to the point of rarely leaving my apartment. I washed the wood floors a lot and grew nice houseplants. I also worked from home; see also: no work friends to speak of. My boyfriend worked in film production and was sometimes away for weeks at a time. We knew one other couple, and then my boyfriend's friendship with one of them fell apart. And then a few months later, I broke up with him.

I can handle isolation. I don't mind it. I can be alone for a stretch. I can call old friends on the phone. But this was crazy. I was basically living and working alone, and I had no one in the entire city of Los Angeles to hang out with. Just going to the corner store felt like an epic journey. I got all bugged out and self-conscious. Like you, I wanted friendships to grow slowly and naturally, and I had no patience for people who seemed too different from me. I was a cross between Winona Ryder in *Heathers* and E.T.—a jumpy, bug-eyed alien life force with a shitty attitude about everyone and everything.

Aww. Poor me!

But even though I was a socially paralyzed shut-in, I realize now that my standards were also way too fucking high. No one was smart enough or interesting enough for me. No one was perfectly equipped to understand every inch of my tortured soul.

Is there any creature alive with higher, more impossible standards than a twenty-eight-year-old? The only difference between a twenty-eight-year-old woman and a thirty-eight-year-old woman is that one of them tries to hide how few friends she has and the other will e-mail you out of the blue and demand to hang out after meeting you for exactly four seconds in a room full of retired people and divorced people and new moms. The late-thirties woman knows that it's no big deal to want to make new friends. Maybe it won't be a life-changing time, or maybe you'll be acquaintances, or maybe you'll be vacationing together down the road. It's worth a shot.

And people past forty? If we get along over the course of an hour's conversation, we practically move in together. We've long since abandoned the dream of 2:00 a.m. curly fries, as well as the luxury of holding out for the exact perfect person to spend time with. We long ago learned to talk to our closest friends on the phone, because they live in Seattle or New York City or fucking Berlin. The rest of the friends we might have in town have kids (if we don't have kids) or they're married (if we're single) or their kids are friends with different kids (if we do have kids), so we have to hang out with whichever motherfuckers happen to have kids in our neighborhood. Our standards are pretty low. Can you carry on a conversation? Is

your kid maybe not a complete asshole? COME SIT NEXT TO
ME; *YOU ARE MY BUDDY.*

So the second thing I want you to know is that in order to
make very close friends in a natural, organic way, you have to
cast a wide net and be accepting and give it time. You can't
use the aggressive, early twentysomething's tactics, because
it poisons the whole process to believe that you're trying to
hunt and trap the perfect BFF. Scrape those curly fries out
of your mind. Some of your closest, lifelong friends may not
seem like close, lifelong friends for the first five or six years
you know them. Seriously. It takes time to figure out who matters, who listens, who tells the truth, who comes through in a
pinch, who's down to earth, who appreciates you and accepts
your flaws, who says the right thing at the right time, and who
makes sense all around.

I get that in your twenties friendships are intertwined
with identity. It can be dangerous to befriend people who are
aggressively different from you, honestly, if your boundaries
are pretty permeable. It's natural to want to stay away from
people who, when you speak honestly about your experiences,
look totally confused or annoyed. But as you get a little older,
you know who you are, and you don't mind knowing people
who don't necessarily get you. Knowing people who don't get
you is good for you, actually. You're exposed to new things,
and you prepare yourself to be a better, more accepting friend,
partner, parent, kid, co-worker—everything. I used to limit
myself to people who were a lot like me. These days, though, I
have friends who are completely different. I have a friend who
reads only romance novels. I have a friend who's a homicide
detective for the LAPD. And I just made a brand-new friend, a
razor-sharp, unapologetically opinionated Frenchwoman who
doesn't eat meat or dairy. I mean, what a waste of Frenchness,
to shun aged cheeses!

I met these people because one friend moved across town,

one friend had a baby, and one friend got too busy with work, so I rarely saw them. One day, I woke up and realized that unless I wanted to be a shut-in, I needed to get out there and fucking make it work. I stuck my neck out and struck up conversations and invited people over. Sometimes I felt sort of pathetic doing it, but I did it anyway.

But the more I made new friends, the clearer it was to me that no one is ever really done making new friends, and very few people are averse to it. I used to assume that people "already had their friends," but that was almost never the case. Even when people seem to be busy and social, they're often very open to getting to know someone new.

And people don't stick to their own categories as much as you'd think. You throw a party or start a book club and people show up, they're curious, they're into it. You go sing karaoke at a bar or go bowling, and everyone is ready to strike up a conversation. They don't care if you're exactly like them. People are friendlier than they seem. It's strange how I didn't understand (or care to recognize) that when I was younger. Interesting people know that interesting people come in all shapes, sizes, and ages.

The ultimate goal is not necessarily to make a bunch of friends who are nothing like you but to get out there and try. You can't be too picky. Open your mind and your heart. Don't stigmatize yourself for having zero friends now. Everyone I know has gone through what you're going through a few times over. Even the perfect social life can evaporate into thin air. The greatest friend group can scatter to the winds overnight. People move and get married and die. Sad, but true.

You've got to get out of that Alone in My Dorm Room, Listening to Other People Laughing on a Saturday Night mentality. You're idealizing other people's lives and friendships because you feel lonely. But the truth is, not that many people are grabbing curly fries at 2:00 a.m., even if they're besties who live together. Other women's lives aren't just one long episode of *Broad City*.

Do you honestly want an uncle who shows up unannounced? Come on. That guy always drops by at dinnertime, and his perpetual-bachelor shtick is no excuse. And have you ever actually *met* a pack of girlfriends who've never celebrated a single birthday without each other? Because those are the kinds of women who insist you wear a tiara out to the bar, demand that you unwrap your birthday presents in front of thirty-two grown adults, and plan painful baby-shower activities that involve sucking on binkies or wearing adult diapers. Maybe these herds make things magical for the birthday girl/bride/pregnant lady, but everyone else in the room is in agony.

You can't get a BFF overnight, and you shouldn't be in the market for that right now anyway. You just need a few people to hang out with every now and then. Mostly, though, you need to practice the art of coming out of your shell, of listening, of making a connection. You can do this with a retiree or a new mom. Maybe it won't amount to anything, but it's still good for you. You can simply exchange a few words, learn something. You can simply show up, hold your own space, feel alive, take in the atmosphere, and be prepared to talk if that situation arises.

You can also invite an awkward ensemble of work friends out for dinner. You can call it "Sushi Thursdays" or "Nacho Night" and fucking dork it out, and people will gobble that shit up. You can start a book club that has one shy work friend, one divorced woman from your knitting group, and one friend of your boyfriend's co-worker in it. You can throw a monthly dinner party and invite people you don't even love that much, just to get back into the practice of listening and getting to know people and putting yourself out there.

I get that these things sound wrong and stupid and maybe not even possible. But you can choose one thing and do it.

The weight of the world doesn't have to rest on this one thing. When I was your age and friendless in L.A., I started running six miles once a week with a doctor friend of my sister's who'd just moved there and didn't know anyone either. The first time he came by my apartment to run, he spotted a copy of *Vanity Fair* with Matt Damon on the cover and said, without irony, "Matt Damon and Ben Affleck—wouldn't you just love to know those guys? I'll bet they'd be really cool to hang out with!"

What could I possibly say to that? I think I went into the kitchen and punched my fist into the wall.

He was a nice guy, though, and after hours of running and talking, we got to be casual friends. He didn't end up being a lifelong friend, but he reminded me that sometimes just being around people, no matter how different they are, feels good. Sometimes it feels good *because* they're totally different from you.

And I think he might've even been right about Damon and Affleck. Who knew?

You will not pull a mother figure or an amazing first cousin or a roomful of lifelong girlfriends out of thin air. Most people don't have those things anyway. We have to fucking make it work instead.

The more you try—without skyrocketing expectations, without circular thoughts that say, "You are a friendless freak!"—the easier it'll be. The more you do it, the happier you'll be. Do it now in order to prepare yourself for doing it twenty years from now, because you'll *always* have to do it. You don't just get the big group of buddies and then sleepwalk through the rest of your life. Life isn't like that.

You have a great life already. You're not starting from zero. You just have to get out of this ashamed, protective place and know that if you work hard to get your head in the right place, people will be drawn to you. You can't get discouraged when great friendships don't appear immediately. You have to keep the faith and keep trying and recognize that it's good for you, and good for everybody else, too. The world is not filled with favorite uncles dropping by packed birthday parties.

As you get older, you notice that some people *do* eventually shut the world out, and other people, the ones who really know how to live, open themselves up and keep meeting new people. My mother, who is seventy-three, has always had a small handful of close friends, and she never went out of her way to meet new people. But then she retired, and her boyfriend died, and one of her lifelong friends died, and after that her dog died. Can you fucking imagine? I've said it before: Being old is a *motherfucker*.

But then, one day, she made two new friends in her neighborhood. Now they go walking together every morning. Sometimes one of them says outrageous, unbelievable things. Sometimes the other one repeats herself. They are not perfect. But they walk and check up on each other and make dinner for each other, drinking cocktails on the back patio together on a warm late-summer evening.

This life is not perfect. This world is not a perfect place. Sometimes it's nice to sip a drink, and repeat yourself, among people who aren't perfect and don't expect you to be perfect either. Aim low, open your heart, and let them in.

Polly

I'm Thirty-Eight and Everything Is Awful

Dear Polly,

I think I'm going down a dark hole, and I could use your help.

A few months ago, I realized I'm thirty-eight. And I started to feel very sad and very afraid. That was on top of already feeling very alone.

Some of this started a long time ago. I lost a parent when I was thirteen, and to this day I am a yawning maw of need. But I learned to hide it well; I overachieved myself to the point of being beyond reproach. How anyone could have believed I was actually okay, let alone ready to make Big Life Decisions about college and the like, is beyond me, but they did. I wasn't. I've been kind of adrift ever since then: lonely, and with only superficial direction to my life that has consisted of always making careful, conservative choices in lieu of having goals or a passion. I always thought I would somehow, someday magically break out of that, but I never did.

Twenty-five years later, I feel I've missed out on a lot. I'm perpetually single (not by choice, but I'm working on "learning to love the process"), I've made many career-based choices that were bad for my personal life (all of which I regret), it's getting harder to relate to my old friends because their lives have changed and mine hasn't, and yes, it's also getting harder to make new friends as I get older. I've been to therapy and have learned to recognize some unproductive habits/patterns, but I can't make up for lost time. I've also found out I have a health condition that exacerbates my natural tendency toward anxiety/depression, and I'm treating it.

Speaking of time, boy, would I love to finally find a partner and have a baby. I don't want to adopt; I want to have a biological baby because it would be related to the parent I lost. I don't want to do it alone. I also don't believe it's going to happen for me, and I'm starting to grieve.

Speaking of grief, I have a small extended family, and they are getting older. None of them live nearby, and the two halves are not in contact with each other. I visit as much as I can, but my job requires a schedule that makes travel difficult, and the nature of the work makes telecommuting impossible on an extended basis. Every time I see them, I feel like it could be the last time.

I'm terribly afraid that I'll be completely alone in the world someday with no partner, no baby, and no extended family. I'm also terribly afraid that I will never LIVE. Most days I just want to sell all of my things and go live in another country for a while so I can, for the first time ever, do something that has an uncertain outcome. I'm ashamed of the reason why I haven't done it: I'm afraid I won't be able to keep saving for retirement, and then what would I do? (More importantly, I'm also afraid I won't be able to visit my family.)

I'm totally paralyzed by all of this fear. How can I use these feelings to do myself some real good for once?

Fear and (Self-)Loathing in the Midwest

—◊◊—

Dear FA(S)LITM,

Reading your letter feels like playing a board game that you can only lose. Every roll of the dice leads to another terrible outcome: Move ahead two spaces and grieve for the baby you never had. Move ahead four spaces and realize you're too old to meet the man of your dreams. Draw an "Unfortunate Twist of Fate" card: "Aging relative enters hospice! Lose your next two turns and pay $30,000." Draw a "Not a Chance in Hell" card: "Advance to Lonely Life Abroad. Do not pass Retirement Savings Bonus, do not collect $100,000."

You are projecting your depressed, anxious, scared past onto your bright and limitless future. I get it (and I've been there), but you have GOT to grab the yoke and pull this plane out of a nosedive. Thirty-eight years old and already grieving for the child you'll never have? Thirty-eight years old and giving up on love, resigning yourself to watch your family fracture and decay without you there, writing off ever living abroad, drawing yourself into a narrower circle each and every day? No. Just NO. You're too young to live this way.

Now, I understand—oh yes I do!—how life can get really dark right around your age. At forty years old, a close friend of mine died of cancer out of the blue, another almost died, my husband had a scary health problem, and I had to accept that I might not live near my mother before she dies (something I've been trying and failing to remedy for almost two decades). Suddenly the rest of my life looked like a slow tumble downward into darkness, punctuated by the deaths of everyone I knew.

And look, it wasn't like I was imagining all of this darkness! It was based on fact. Hitting age forty means accepting your limitations, your own decline, and the decline of EVERYONE YOU FUCKING KNOW. If you don't accept it, you'll feel even worse. This is why we oldish people buy so many books about aging and dying. Because our culture won't let us admit that we're going to fall apart slowly and then die, so we have to find ways to face it on our own.

But facing the truth doesn't have to induce misery. Once you mourn your carefree youth and give yourself some time to adjust to the reality of your adulthood, that's when happiness begins. You take it all in, and you say, "Holy god, the path ahead looks deeply awful and terrifying to me!" Then you get off your ass and make your life as good as it can possibly be TODAY.

If you can't manage that, if you're buried by the darkness, that means you're probably battling low-grade depression and anxiety and negative self-talk to boot, and you have to tirelessly address those factors until it's actually possible to be a little optimistic. If I were you, I would redouble my efforts on that front—with healthier habits from top to bottom—while simultaneously encouraging optimism in yourself as much as you can. You have to speak to yourself in a kind way. I know that sounds absurd, but basically you have to say things like "Look at you and your early morning writing! Good job, sunshine!" and "Hey, you fit in a workout and ate a healthy breakfast. Way to take care of yourself!" Dorky but cumulatively more effective than you can imagine. And honestly, I don't know a better way to battle existential angst and fear than by seizing each day by the throat and forcing it into a shape that feels productive and healthy and on track. You do not sit around bemoaning the big picture, day in and day out. NO. You focus on charging forward, on becoming a better, healthier, more generous, more balanced sort of a person; you call your friends and your family to talk often; you give of yourself; and you resolve to do that again and again, every second of every goddamn day until they come and grab your dead body and shove it into a coffin.

Because, guess what? When you're over forty, you have to work a hundred times harder to just exist and breathe and feel good. It's not JUST that you can't sleep four hours at night or drink way too much. Most of us ALSO can't eat hamburgers whenever, we can't stop exercising or we get headaches and feel like death warmed over. We can't let our Bad Brains take over and ruin everything anymore. We have to feel our feelings, yes, and we also have to push our feelings aside long enough to run five miles.

You're thirty-eight years old. I know you're trying to fix a lot of things. But you have time.

Here's what I would do if I were you, and many will disagree with me: I would focus on finding a great partner. I really would. I think you can whip yourself into a better emotional state and do this at the same time. It will be challenging, but I think if you're optimistic and in a state of forward motion, you'll find that rapport with others comes easily. Open your heart and hurl yourself out there and refuse to slice and dice every single date; just cast a wide net and see what happens.

I would also consider having a kid on my own. I would simply look into it, without freaking out. I would gather information.

I would not move abroad at this moment. I would leave that as a reward—at, say, age forty-two or so—if you haven't met anyone great and/or you decide against having a kid and maybe a few relatives die so you're free and clear.

See how cavalier I'm being? That's how you need to be about this for a while. You know why? You're getting older, you want a kid, you want a guy, you're running out of time, and people die eventually. These are the facts on the ground. They aren't going to change. Dive in and work with them instead of allowing yourself to fill up with fear and sadness until you're paralyzed.

In short, there's an overarching existential dance you have to learn. It's a combination of accepting your own death and doing the very best to live at your maximum capacity today and every day. You know what you want. That's the good part. Now you have to walk out the door and get it. If you sit around preemptively mourning the fact that you'll never get what you want, guess what? YOU WILL NEVER GET WHAT YOU WANT.

Will you get what you want? I don't know, but if I were you, I would build it into my belief system. I WILL LIVE THE LIFE I WANT. Maybe you'll have to make adjustments. Maybe you'll have a kid alone or not have a kid at all. Cross that bridge when you come to it, but resolve to cross it with optimism, marching or dancing a little as you go.

It's the only way. Don't lament and worry endlessly. Don't let yourself spin in circles over your dreary big picture. Resolve to do the best you can with what you have. Resolve to play a board game that you can only win. Every roll of the dice leads to another great outcome: Move ahead two spaces and celebrate the freedom of being child-free by moving to Berlin! Move ahead four spaces and meet your soul mate! Draw an "Amazing Twist of Fate" card: "Aging relative enters hospice! Lose your next four turns and have one of the richest, saddest experiences of your life"! Draw a "You Never Fucking Know" card: "Advance to Incredible New Lease on Life. Collect lasting friendships and companionship from every player"!

I know you've got to reprogram yourself from the ground up and that will take a lot of work. I also know that you're up for the challenge. This is just what people do as they near forty. They finally figure things out, and then they enter the best days of their lives. Join us! It's not over till it's over, motherfuckers.

Polly

Don't Shy Away

Dear Polly,

I've never really been good at socializing. As a child, I was nerdy, quiet, and independent. I was happier spending recess following a trail of ants than interacting with classmates. In high school, I was a loner who was utterly confused by the complexity of social interaction. I found the Internet a more rewarding avenue, where small talk was unnecessary and I could easily pick and choose from interesting conversations instead of working with the people I happened to be around in real time.

And so I never really learned. The Internet was my social life for most of my twenties. By an astounding stroke of luck, I met a woman who lived nearby who was amazing and liked me. We fell in love and cohabited for eight years. But my lack of social skills wore on our relationship. We never really communicated, and I was oblivious to the need. What more is there to say than "I love you"? Eventually, she came to interpret this obliviousness as a lack of caring, and she started resenting me. By the time she spoke up, it was too late. A year of couples counseling and hard work on my part yielded nothing; she told me, "I'm afraid you are just not capable of connecting with people."

I was devastated. Flattened. Erased. But I used it. I changed everything about my life. I made socializing a priority. No degree of awkwardness could ever come close to hurting as much as I already did. I was strangely optimistic. I was free from a relationship that wasn't working, and I was free from inhibitions that had held me back. I threw myself into it, went out four or five times a week, engaged strangers in small talk, made a lot of friends, picked up an instrument, got asked to join the board of a nonprofit, got invited to parties, threw parties of my own, and put a lot of effort into being interesting and attractive to others. It's been amazingly rewarding in ways I never knew possible.

And yet there's still something that's not working. Despite having lots of friends, I have no close ones. My conversations still feel stilted; they don't flow. The mechanical nature of small talk is something that can be practiced and learned, but the easy, free-flowing give-and-take that really connects people eludes me entirely. I see people do it; I don't know how it's done. And flirting? I don't even know where to start.

So when I try to date, it's the same thing every time. I'm reasonably attractive, employed, intelligent, and unafraid of failure. So I start off pretty strong. I get obvious interest when I approach women and try to be engaging. But inevitably, the conversation falls flat after two or three exchanges. Once I run out of "Have you seen this band before?" and "That beer looks good, how is it?" I don't know what to say. Online dating is no better. With the buffer of a keyboard and time to think, I can be pretty verbose and articulate. (I'm sure you've noticed.) So I get a lot of first dates, almost no second dates, and after a year of effort zero third dates.

I've seen therapists regarding this issue. Universally, they treat it as anxiety. No one seems to understand that it's a lack of words and not the fear of saying them. It's more like writer's block than stage fright. I have no problem giving lectures, explaining technical issues, asking questions. When it's obvious that data need to be exchanged for some practical purpose, I can speak all day. But just plain chatting eludes me entirely. How do I know when I should be saying something? What should I say? Anything? How do I choose one thing to say?

I'm really frustrated and losing hope. I need someone to love. I know I have a lot to offer a partner, but I'm getting no takers. I would be okay with this if I knew what to do. If I had exercises I could do that would improve the skills I'm missing. I'm beginning to feel that my ex was right. That I don't just lack skills, but that I have a fundamental inability to relate to people in a way that makes them want to get close to me. I've found that I love people, but I'm terrible at interacting with them. Am I just broken and undatable? Can I be fixed? How?

Too Shy

—⚬—

Dear Too Shy,

First of all, let's acknowledge that lots of people don't get third dates these days. Something has gone wrong in the online dating universe lately, and now courting has become this barren landscape of snap judgments, baked by a relentless sun of suspicion and whipped by the prevailing winds of dissatisfaction, until nothing but hostility and disappointment can grow. Instead of looking for areas of connection, people scrutinize each other for flaws.

But people are flawed, the end! You can't *be* a people without being flawed. Pretending otherwise and looking for perfection in others is a path of self-hatred and delusion and mutual lifelong bullshitting.

All of this reflects a wider societal shift toward encountering anyone who seems even slightly out of step with the reigning cultural ideal of cool indifference as damaged goods. People who are anxious or pensive or a tiny bit off-kilter are quickly labeled as losers or freaks. People who are shy or conversationally awkward or just out of practice are written off as shut-ins or nerds. The irony is that apathy and vagueness and underexplaining and fading out—attitudes and behaviors that drive the sensitive among us insane—are defined as normal. Remember how people used to say that this or that social scene "is just like high school all over again"? Well, the whole world is high school all over again. We are expected to act like cool kids— light, breezy, disengaged—in every environment. As a culture, we're unknowingly mimicking carefully scripted sitcom characters, as if they represent some Platonic ideal of humanity. We expect ourselves and each other to move through the world with the bulletproof, professionally slick, faux confidence of comedic sidekicks and superheroes.

And who can navigate the world with such disingenuous suaveness? (1) Deeply insecure humans who've worked very, very hard to shield themselves in a high gloss of fake to obscure their doubts about themselves; (2) actors (See also No. 1); and (3) people with layers and layers of hurt and pain that they haven't explored, who don't understand themselves, and who don't give a fuck about anyone but themselves. We are unknowingly privileging insecure pricks, narcissists, actors, liars, and fakes, while regular, humble, gently worn humans get kicked to the curb.

So. I could feed you the basics of casual comedic-sidekick-style flirtation. Or you could take instruction from one of a million self-proclaimed pickup artists. But your central problem will remain. As difficult as these interactions are for you right now, you need to recognize that YOU are not, strictly speaking, the problem. It's not your responsibility to keep these conversations afloat. The only difference between you and some jack-juice who keeps women interested is that HE rests comfortably in the pauses in the conversation. He doesn't mind just sitting there, allowing for some dead air, while he stares into the middle distance. He's not afraid of looking at a date like "Okay, that's all I've got. How about you?" He's not questioning everything he says every step of the way. So you don't need a better script. What you need is some practice doing LESS. You need to learn to forget yourself in the moment, to relax and take in the scenery without trying to make everything right. Practice not firing off questions and filling in the gaps. Let a woman think that you're a little bit reserved sometimes. That's not a turnoff. Fumbling for the next conversation piece after three dates, that's a turnoff.

That's the close-up of your situation. But if you zoom out, there's a larger problem. The larger problem is that you believe that there's something wrong with you. And as long as you believe that, you'll struggle with these situations.

I don't think there's anything wrong with you. You're a little bit awkward, and maybe you haven't had enough close friendships to know what goes on in other people's heads and hearts. Maybe you can't relate to other people that easily. You could hardly be expected to have drilled down into the depths of your long-term girlfriend's psyche after eight years of mumbling to each other about surface shit. She had built-up resentments by the end, and her feelings faded. It happens.

But I don't think you need to fundamentally change the way you talk to people just to find someone to love. I do think, though, that you need to understand who you are and know what matters to you before you move forward.

Because even though people are shallow and lots of people prefer scripted fictional heroes to real human beings, they *can* still be shaken out of it in the presence of someone who is REAL. Your problem is not that you haven't mastered the conversational skills necessary to maintain someone's interest. Your problem is that you've never forced yourself to define exactly who you are and what you love and how you want to live. You've never had to talk about these things passionately. You've never dared to lay yourself bare, without apology. Once you can look someone in the eyes and say, "Here's what really matters to me"? That's what people find attractive, trust me. They want to be with someone who knows himself and gives a shit. That's what's alluring and attractive and irreplaceable, even in this age of smooth make-believe.

Because anyone can master the conversational arts, or flirting, or negging, or acting the part. That's easy enough to do. That's like memorizing your multiplication tables. Go ahead and do it if it gets you out of your slump. But understanding yourself at a deeper level is like mastering conceptual math. It's more gratifying and more interesting—and look, you're a smart, able-bodied human. You're up for the challenge, aren't you?

I think you should stop dating for a while. Focus on yourself instead. Go see a therapist and dig into your earliest memories, what makes you tick, what you want from your life, what you expect from love. Dig in and figure out who you are. Keep a journal and write down your thoughts every morning and every night. Listen to music while you write if that helps you to access your emotions more easily.

While you're doing this, train your social energies on enriching your friendships. Think about what it would take to have closer friendships with people. Would you have to see each other more often for camaraderie and familiarity to build? Would you need to have lunch or dinner so you could sit across from each other and talk? What if you hosted a weekly poker game with the same people every week, women and men? What if you tried to go out to a movie with a friend once a month? Casual friendships grow into close friendships with repeated exposure, so allow it to happen. Accumulate experience together. As you each open up, trust will build.

I think that for now close friends are the answer—male and female. You need to make some connections that go beyond casual hanging out. You have to allow time for people to reveal themselves to you, and you have to start revealing yourself— first to yourself and then to others. You need to learn what it feels like to be completely relaxed and unguarded in someone else's company.

Love blooms more easily among people who understand intimacy and trust with close friends. When you can tell a close friend the truth about your feelings and your insecurities and your flaws, when you can make a joke about them and your friend can tease you and you can feel seen and known and understood, that's—well, it's a kind of love. Casual friendship is nothing compared with that.

Which of your friendships have potential to blossom that way? What kinds of clubs or group activities might you join that would expose you to people who might interest you?

Meet some new people. Forget the small talk. Practice asking big questions and listening to the answers. Practice NOT filling up the pauses in conversation with empty words. Practice being comfortable with silence. Practice paying less attention to how you're coming across. Focus on the other person instead. Stay attuned to his emotions, the meaning behind what he says. Does he seem lonely? Does she feel isolated? Does he feel dissatisfied?

Maybe you can't relate to people that well now, but you will in time. You have to be present, though. You have to forget yourself and take in the layers of experience that are buzzing around you. The smart people around you will tolerate some awkwardness for the sake of knowing someone else who's smart and interesting. But if you don't know who you are and what you're all about, if you're ashamed and distracted by the nervous noise in your head, you won't be able to take part in the beauty of the world around you.

So you have some work to do. Luckily, you don't mind working hard. Get to know yourself well. Get to know other people well. Forget the sitcom characters and the superheroes and realize your full potential as a lovable, sensitive, gently worn human being. Be patient but keep the faith. Because, trust me, eventually, some great woman out there is going to be thrilled to find you.

Polly

I Don't Know

Dear Polly,

What I get from your column is to be truthful and open and honest with yourself. And find yourself and love yourself. But can I just say this? I don't know. I don't fucking know. I just have no idea. I am twenty-five years old and I live in an apartment and it's good, I guess. I don't know; I guess it's good. I go to yoga and that's good; I guess I like yoga. I think I like yoga. I do. But what do I really like about it? I like how it makes my body feel and look.

I have a job and it's pretty good, I guess. I don't know. I guess it's good. I make money. I'm okay at it. I'm not the best, but I want to be the best, but I can't be and I won't be. I'm not smart and good enough . . . I don't know. I know I should think I'm smart, but come on. I'm smart, I guess. I don't know. I see my friends. I fantasize about warm summer nights and beautiful sunsets and buildings against a clear sky on a cold winter evening and magical moments that kind of happen but sorta don't.

But I don't know. I answer people with "I don't know." I second-guess myself all the time. If you ask me a question I'll say "I think . . ." or "Let me double check" or "I don't know," because I just don't know anything. Will I ever know? Will I ever know and be certain about something? Will it ever just click into place and I'll know? I'll know it's right?

I Don't Know

—w—

Dear IDK,

I don't always know either. Part of what I like about giving people advice is that I never fucking know how I'm going to pull it off. I'm not some kind of swami or guru. I don't have the answers to everything. Half of the time I sit down and draw a complete blank. But I know that by the end of a few pages, I *have* to know. I have to or I won't have a column to send to my editor. I love this job because every goddamn week I have to know *something*.

I love feeling my way in the dark, grasping into the void for the things that make sense to me. And I love looking back on difficult times in my life when I felt like I didn't know anything and remembering what that felt like. It makes me feel grateful to do that.

Because I was like you for more than a decade. I wasn't sure about anything. I had friends whom I liked just fine and a job I liked most of the time. I used to *say* that I felt grateful for my job, but I didn't really *feel* grateful; I just knew that I *should* feel grateful for it. I had a boyfriend who was nice; I thought I was probably lucky to have him. I didn't always feel lucky, though. So I got a new boyfriend, and I felt a little bit luckier, but I still didn't really know.

I wasn't sure what the future held for me. I used to say that I wasn't very ambitious. I knew I wanted to have a house and some kids, but *just* having a house and some kids sounded pretty terrible, really. I loved my new boyfriend, but I wasn't sure he'd make a very good husband. Being married to him sounded pretty terrible, too. But maybe that was just me being negative. I wasn't sure.

I asked other people's opinions a lot back then. No one seemed to know what I should do about anything. They all said stuff like "Well, how do *you* feel about it?" Sometimes I would tell them what I thought about things, and then I'd just get lost in a long analysis of my thoughts, and everyone would end up feeling bored and annoyed, myself included. My aunt once said to me, "You just told me what you *think*. Now tell me how you *feel*." I said, "How I feel? Is there a difference?" She told me yes, there's a big difference. So I thought about how I felt for a minute. I didn't know how I felt, though. I didn't know how I felt about anything.

The closest things that felt like feelings to me were more like longings: I wanted a grassy backyard with a comfortable lounge chair in it. I wanted to sip a cold beer and eat raw oysters and watch the sunset. I wanted to feel loved and safe. I wanted to be beautiful, to be surrounded by beautiful things. I wanted to feel proud of myself.

So I get where you're coming from. When I look back now, I see someone who felt plenty of things but never really trusted her own feelings to guide her: I would daydream about meeting a better boyfriend, but I wouldn't dump my not-all-that-great one. I would be plagued by the feeling that I was wasting my time at my job, but I wouldn't quit. I would blow off my friends when I felt wronged by them, but I wouldn't tell them when they neglected me or hurt my feelings.

I didn't feel my feelings that much, because I was worried that if I did, I would fall apart and I'd quit my job and I'd dump my boyfriend and I'd be totally depressed. I didn't trust myself to fix things in my own life, and I was afraid of being alone. I wanted to avoid making any rash decisions about anything, because that way at least I would feel safe and secure and nothing would have to change.

I also didn't trust myself, because I was mad at myself all the time. Everything I did was some kind of fuckup. I woke up too late. My hair looked like shit. My face was breaking out. I wasn't lovable. I left a mess in the kitchen the night before. I hadn't exercised for a few days. These things were all my fault.

The bad voice in my head said, "Oh my god. What are you doing *now*? Come on, get your shit together!"

These terrible cognitive habits essentially coached me into never feeling my feelings. Any feeling that came up meant that I was weak and stupid. "You're seriously going to cry about your kitchen being a mess? What a pathetic person you are!" my head would say when I started to feel sorry for myself. Even though, thanks to therapy, I'd gone through brief periods of trying to welcome in emotions without judgment, I couldn't manage to do it regularly. If I felt very angry or very sad, that could only mean that I was about to scare away my boyfriend and my family and whatever remaining friends I had. I didn't believe that anyone would ever love me as long as I let my emotions out and felt vulnerable.

So I was in a defensive, self-attacking stance for a long time. That's where I think your particular kind of wishy-washy, ambivalent "I don't know" comes from, IDK. It comes from negative self-talk, and it comes from having powered down your emotions, either in the wake of some trauma or just as a result of having chided yourself for having emotions at all for many years. Maybe emotions weren't welcome in your family. Or maybe at some point, you subconsciously latched onto the belief that your emotions were the enemy and they would fuck up your entire life if you didn't put a lid on them.

Lots of people believe that, and there are a wide range of negative side effects that flow forth from that belief. "I don't know" might seem like a relatively minor side effect, but I think it might mean that you're mildly depressed.

Don't take the word "mildly" mildly here! Being mildly depressed can fuck with your life on every level. It keeps you from feeling great at work or feeling exhilarated after a great yoga class. It turns you into someone who's always peering into someone else's windows, wondering why the people inside seem so passionate and happy and thrilled, wondering if they're just simpleminded or stupid, wondering if they grew up in happier homes so they're not damned to shuffle around in a haze of uncertainty the way that you are.

In order to KNOW—and yes, I definitely think things will click into place and you *will* know something at some point— you have to excavate a little. You have to see a therapist and dig for the reasons why you've stopped feeling your own feelings, happiness and sadness and sweetness and anger alike. You also have to train yourself not to give yourself a hard time about every goddamn thing under the sun.

In addition to seeing a therapist, you should try very hard to notice how you talk to yourself throughout the course of the day. I'm going to guess, based on your letter, that you often tell yourself that you'll never be smart enough or good enough at work. You tell yourself that you are missing something that the smart, successful people at your job have. You tell yourself that you're too wishy-washy to ever be a huge success, to ever be loved and adored by anyone, to ever have close, loving friends. You are inherently flawed in tragic ways. You will never amount to shit.

Listen to these messages, and marvel at them. Marvel at how many times a day you tell yourself that you suck. Don't marvel and say, "Jesus, all of this self-talk about how I suck is EVEN MORE PROOF OF HOW MUCH I SUCK!" No. Marvel that you do this, and marvel that *so many other people* do this around the clock, for their entire lives.

You'll be staring at one source of your wishy-washiness. You'll be taking it in. Don't stop! Keep noticing. And after a few weeks of noticing, when you hear that voice that says, "Oh my god, you fucking idiot," in your head, follow it up with another voice. "Am I an idiot just because I didn't do the dishes? Or do I not *want* to do the dishes. Is that really a crime?"

Likewise, when you are at yoga class, pay attention. Do you tell yourself that you're mediocre at yoga the whole time? Or do you look inside for your feelings. Do you do a stretch and think, "Christ, this hurts! I am so inflexible still!" Or do you think, "I am here, trying. I am a person who tries. I do what I fucking can. It's okay to just try."

Once you start accepting yourself in your self-talk, you may find yourself feeling overcome, literally bursting into tears. THAT IS A BEAUTIFUL FUCKING THING! Let yourself burst into tears. Say to yourself, "I am feeling really sad right now, and weak, and lost, and that's not just okay; it's good. It's exactly how I need to feel in this moment. This sadness doesn't make me weak. This is what it feels like *not* to be wishy-washy. This is me, finding my way in the dark. This is how I'll finally know something, by recognizing how lost I feel, by recognizing how little I know now."

It sounds paradoxical, but uncertainty and vulnerability are your guides through this soggy life you're living. Leaning into your not knowing will bring you more knowledge and wisdom and understanding than you ever dreamed of.

But even once you know a lot, and everything clicks into place, and you feel like you're on the right path and you really *feel* for the people around you and for the life you've created, you'll still have to remind yourself that you are vulnerable and unsure at your core. You'll still need to welcome in your so-called negative emotions when they come rushing at you. If they never come rushing at you, don't be afraid to go looking for them.

You'll go looking for them so you don't ever power everything down again, or shut people out again, or feel wishy-washy and angry at yourself and not good enough again.

The bottom line is that being truthful and open and honest with yourself means letting in those scary emotions and noticing the angry self-talk and embracing all of it. That turmoil, that fear, that anger, that self-hatred, and that sadness will be your guide. It will—very slowly, the more you embrace it—guide you to who you are and what you love. Follow your uncertainty and fear into the darkness, accept that the darkness will always be a part of you, and recognize that that's where you'll find your passions. Then you'll finally KNOW.

And sometimes you won't know, too. But it won't feel the same as the "I don't know" that haunts you now. It will be a new kind of "I don't know" that helps you close your eyes, to feel how good it is to be alive, to feel how good it is to just breathe. It's an "I don't know" that also says to you, "I am just a person, and I don't have any answers. I will never have all of the answers. My job is simply to try." You don't need a fantasy (sunset, true love, giant piles of cash). You don't need to be surer of your talents.

Every morning, you will wake up and see that life is all about fumbling and *accepting* that you're fumbling. It's about saying nice things to yourself, even when you're lazy, even when you're lost. It's about giving yourself the love you need in order to try—JUST TRY—so that someday you'll have enough love to give a little to someone else.

Life is not about knowing. Life is about feeling your way through the dark. If you say, "This should be lighter by now," you're shutting yourself off from your own happiness. So let there be darkness. Get down on your knees, and crawl through the dark. Crawl and say to yourself, "Holy GOD, it's dark, but just look at me crawl! I can crawl like a *motherfucker*."

Polly

Career or Baby?

Dear Polly,

I am a twenty-seven-year-old woman happily married for the last two years, living in a great home. I've been actively building the life I've always dreamed of, but I have a steady corporate job at a bank, which I feel absolutely nothing for. What's worse, my manager retired and I hate my new boss, so my easy, secure job is now the seventh circle of hell. Every day, I dread walking into my building and feel like a total failure who is wasting away her life with every passing heartbeat.

Now I only want to start a family. But I feel that if I do, I will never go back to work, nor will I figure out what I want to do with myself careerwise. I'm looking for a new job at the same company, but my heart isn't in it, because I'm not interested in the industry and I'd still be an anonymous and invisible employee of an enormous corporation. But I'm afraid of leaving because this job has great benefits, especially when it comes to maternity leave. I would leave for a "dream job," but I have no idea what that is. My real dream is to be the parent who works from home or for herself.

As far as careers go, I can see myself as an interior designer, or in the hospitality industry, or maybe as some kind of broadcast journalist. I am creative, and I love to write. I often consider going back to school for broadcast journalism (a four-year program), but I will surely be pregnant by/before graduation. And then what, the degree goes on hold while I build my family? I read a lot about women and careers and feel that by now I should have a job I can "lean in" to so that when I bow out and become a parent, I have a good career foundation established. I also feel that if I want to have any semblance of a career while juggling family, I should probably be pregnant yesterday so that I'll only be in my forties when my kids are eighteen. I have considered starting a small business I could handle part-time, but I can't invest the time since I only have evenings and weekends to get anything done.

I feel plagued by all the things I should be doing with my career life before getting pregnant. Should I move on to a different, less-shitty corporate job, then get pregnant? Should I take the time to really figure out what I want to do for work, then pursue it fully? Should I quit my job to set up a small side business before I'm pregnant or invest in this venture only on evenings and weekends? Should I just get pregnant soon-ish, roll the dice, see where the career chips fall?

My husband works for small companies, and we rely on my job for the banking perks and job security, but he's supportive of anything I wish to do. He just wants me to decide and to commit. I have no idea what to decide, and I am so scared of committing. I have asked this same question to my friends, peers, elders, and family. Everyone's answer varies: (1) Don't get pregnant while you hate your job, you'll be so hormonal and emotional, and pregnancy is supposed to be a happy time; (2) get pregnant while you're at this job, and milk it for all it's worth; (3) quit your job altogether, and find out what you want to do.

No one understands the variables—that we cannot afford to lose my job, that I need to work here until I have something new, that I don't actually give a fuck about finding something new, because I don't want to work, I want to be at home with babies. I feel like it's a crime to say this out loud. I feel judged and judge myself harshly when I say this. I am a smart and capable woman who should have a meaningful career, and if I don't, I'm not a smart, capable woman; I'm just a parent. I feel so much pressure to be the career woman who has it all, I worry that by having a family I'll never have a career, and I feel plagued by the fact that I don't honestly care enough about building a career, because all I want is to make a beautiful home and raise a beautiful family with my beautiful husband. But then, in ten years, maybe I will regret not having been more career focused.

All I do is imagine other women's lives and wonder how they managed it all. More than anything, I am paralyzed by fear. I can't even address what pregnancy and childbearing themselves would mean to my marriage, my body, my house, my mental health. I wish I did not have to multitask or juggle all this. I wish I was allowed to just be a woman who wants to get pregnant, I wish I could trust myself to figure it all out, I wish I could stop judging myself, I wish I had even an inkling as to which to choose—career or baby?

Help!
Career or Baby

—⁕—

Dear Career or Baby,

It looks like you've unknowingly stumbled on the mantra of the working mother. Akin to Bill Murray's nihilistic rallying cry of "It just doesn't matter!" from *Meatballs,* the working mother repeats to herself, over and over, "There is no satisfactory solution!" It's one part "There's no place like home!" and two parts "There's no milk in the fridge, and I'm on deadline!"

At this very minute, in fact, my husband is across the country at a conference, and I am sitting next to a pile of ten books I need to read for various assignments. My kids are at a friend's house, but they'll be home soon, and they wrote "park" and "tee party" on the calendar for the day. See? There is no satisfactory solution. Go to the park and have a tea party and worry about work the whole time, or make the kids play by themselves all afternoon and feel like a neglectful mother? As a working parent, you often feel like you have to choose between neglecting your career or spending too little time with your kids. You're always burning the candle at both ends, pissing into the wind, and robbing the cat to pay the dog.

But—casting aside the feminist layers of this issue for a moment—this state of affairs is not impossible and terrible and lamentable, necessarily. It's simply WHAT IT FEELS LIKE TO HAVE IT ALL.

Because having it all, by its very nature, implies that you have a lot more than you can handle. Who can handle "it all," anyway? "ALL" IS A WHOLE FUCKING HELL OF A LOT. If you have some kids and a career and you don't have big piles of cash and a staff of five, you're going to be busier and more conflicted than you've ever been before. Okay, even with the money and the staff, you'll be busy and conflicted.

So why not just say fuck the career and have the baby? Why not just say to hell with kids and pursue a career you love instead? Why try to have "it all" at all? Here's why: Because having a great career is the best and having babies is fucking incredible and having both is AMAZING, and no, I'm not kidding, not even a little bit.

Choose both. Choose the career, AND choose the baby. Don't put off one for the other. Choose both now and later, and accept that you'll be juggling for years no matter what you do. Even if you never have a career, you're going to feel like you're juggling. Parents juggle. Why not juggle things you love? Sure, you'll have to work hard and make some sacrifices. Accept it and move forward.

Because even though you keep saying you "don't want to work," you "just want to have beautiful babies," I read that as the temporary sentiment of someone who's trapped in a job she hates. I know plenty of happy housewives, but they're naturally low-key people for the most part, not people who send rambling three-page letters to advice columnists. Based on the racing, anxious rhythms of your letter, I really don't think you fit the happy-housewife profile. I think you're imagining that "downshifting" to raise beautiful babies is a little bit like an extended vacation, a little breast-feeding and cooing and one gorgeous photo op after another. If your husband and maybe an in-law are around after the baby is born (strongly recommend!), your maternity leave will feel luxurious and relaxing. But day-to-day life at home alone with an infant is a particular kind of challenge, one that, based on my personal observations, suits maybe one out of ten women well. I love babies a lot, but I need a little bit of time each day to think and write and be alone and get shit done. It's easy enough to get obsessed with having babies when you love your husband, love your house, hate your job, and don't know what else you'd want to do instead. But I would strongly recommend that you not make the choice to have a baby sooner simply because it offers the best one-way ticket away from corporate purgatory.

You need to address your career situation separately instead of throwing it into the mix of having kids. You already know for a fact that you don't want a job in corporate banking. That's never going to change. I would make a plan to quit within the next year. I would make a plan to save money and scale back your spending. I would commit to exercising once a day, to keep your spirits up and tackle your anxious nature. I would put your ideas about your new career on paper. I would talk to people who do what you want to do for a living. I would take action, and yes, maybe dedicate nights and weekends to figuring it out.

Okay, and what is this horseshit about keeping your job for the banking perks? The fact that you even put those words to paper tells me that you aren't seeing clearly. Do you want to wake up five years from now and say to yourself, "Well, I was miserable for a long time, but fuck, those banking perks were really something"?

You have to stay calm and practical, and you have to move forward, one step at a time. You know what you want already: You want a career, you want a baby, and you want a job you can do from home. You also mention broadcast journalism, but honestly that particular route sounds like a stressful crapshoot for you given your strong desire to have a family soon. Four years of school and then you're either a local anchor or you're traveling for stories, or else you're sitting at home with babies, looking at your degree on the wall? (This is obviously my personal take on it, but most people won't give you any kind of opinion on a job you might want to do, so I'm going to step up to the plate and Be That Asshole.) This doesn't sound like a good fit for you given your current desire for a good work/life balance, nor does it sound like some kind of lifelong dream you'll die if you don't pursue. If it is, then disregard everything I've written here, and fucking go for it.

It's understandable but also a big mistake to read fifteen thousand articles about How Women Can't Have It All and then think yourself into a deep dark hole over how you'll ever pull it off. In this case—and so many others—fixating on the Big Picture will only drag you under. The hysteria around these choices is off the charts. People will say, "Oh, lots of parents regret having kids; they just don't tell you about it." Or, "Working women are miserable," or "Kids with working mothers are anxious and unhappy," or "Kids will destroy your career," or "If you can't give your children every ounce of your energy, you shouldn't have kids at all," or "You can't be a real artist and have kids," and all kinds of other completely black-and-white, fearful, conflicted nonsense. I'm not inside other people's heads, but the close friends I have who are in good marriages (like yours) and have kids AND engaging careers are some of the happiest people I know.

So, listen, you'll deal with problems as they come up. The problems come up every day, and the problems change every millisecond. Babies and toddlers are two different species of animal, and schoolkids are in some ways more high maintenance than either. There will be countless challenges along the way, and there will be plenty of solutions, too. Some of them might even feel satisfactory for a second or two.

Another thing: Being pregnant makes you irritable and ambitious at the same time. Use that energy to fuel your new business. Once you stop feeling hungover around the clock, you're going to want to conquer new terrain and strangle anyone who tells you to "relax." During my first pregnancy, I channeled this energy into writing scathing TV reviews. During my second pregnancy, I wrote a book; I couldn't sleep, so I woke up at 4:00 in the morning and wrote. I know this vision is just as idealistic and misleading as any other and every story is different. But I just want you to know that I, personally, was amazed at how much more energetic I was as a pregnant lady. I often said to my husband, "Whatever this drug is, I wish I could take it FOREVER." (Then I probably said something like, "Go get me some nachos, or I'll bust in your kneecaps with this tire iron.")

Save now to hire a nanny if your husband can't take paternity leave. And don't say, "Women have been dealing with infants on their own for centuries." Women have been treated like chattel for centuries, too. Living in a village full of women is a far cry from haunting a house in the suburbs with an adorable little alien who turns into a screaming banshee for mysterious reasons every few hours. Find a way to get help. Find a way. LOTS of help. The biggest mistake new mothers make is telling themselves, "I should be able to handle this all by myself." Bullshit. You should do what you need to do to take care of yourself and not send yourself off a fucking cliff emotionally. Babies have no use for parents whose nerves are frayed to the point of no return, and babies are biologically designed to fray nerves like a motherfucker because it guarantees that their needs will get met.

So, look, I could write an entire book on this subject—a terrible, highly subjective book. Most parents could. All I want to tell you is that you can have a baby and have a career and yes, I think it's very smart to want both and to go for both. Should you wait to have the baby? Maybe set up the business and get it going first, yes. I wouldn't wait that long—either to quit or to start your business or to have babies. I don't think you should get overly strategic about the timing of kids. It's great to have a good marriage and know what you want when you're young and full of steam. But for those who aren't there yet, I'm forty-five and I have a seven-year-old, and that's great, too. My husband and I both have established, flexible careers, and that makes parenting feel much less exhausting and lonely. There are advantages and disadvantages to every timeline.

Bottom line: I was fearful, but throwing my energy into both my kids and my career turned out so much better than I ever thought it would. I became much more focused and ambitious after I had kids. I valued my time more. I used my time more wisely. All of the time I used to spend questioning myself and worrying about the big picture is now spent doing dishes and folding little dresses. A lot of the working mothers I know feel the same way.

You're smart and ambitious, and you're sensitive to feeling like you're wasting your time. You sound like someone who will need to work at least part-time for the rest of your life, particularly once you find something that you really enjoy. Don't confuse your current lame job with the feeling of working at something that feels gratifying to you, where you complete projects from start to finish instead of just punching a clock every day. Imagine a full life, and be true to that vision. Defend it. And put fear aside. You have one person with a steady job in the house. Don't panic. Look closely at your budget, and make it work. (And go read *The Two-Income Trap* while you're at it.)

You *can* have it all. You may have to adjust the particulars of "IT," but trust me, "ALL" is what you want. It's exhausting and it's a balancing act and it's way too much for anyone to handle, ever. That's also what's so gratifying about it.

Polly

VII

Beauty in the Breakdown

I Feel Haunted by My Affair

Hi, Polly,

I'd like to first say that I find your advice more than just good but revelatory and sort of almost mystical. Which is why I'm writing to you, half-drunk on a Saturday morning, about one of the things that has been most leaving me reaching for prescriptions lately.

I'm a very long-married person in her early forties. By very long, I mean we started dating when we were eighteen, were married a whole seven years later.

We have had all the problems that people who marry young have, by which I mean sexual foundering and infidelity. While we both have red in our ledger, I have been the guiltier party. But we've always had a rapport and love and understanding that managed to overcome it, with the help of a little therapy.

But.

Five years ago, I had dinner with a guy. A semi-famous guy, whom I had long deeply admired. I had no notion that I was sexually attracted to him, but at the end of that (husband-approved) dinner things went haywire. It was a onetime thing, and we kept up occasional, friendly, every-once-in-a-while-sexy contact over the next years. Until a few weeks ago, when he texted me because he was in town from L.A.—now graduated from semi- to super-famous—and we met again.

And it was something I can't even describe. I don't really think it's about the fame thing, though I could be deluding myself on that score. It was a few hours in a hotel room, but I felt seen and listened to in this way that I feel like I've never been.

The sex rocked. But that's not the big takeaway. It was feeling . . . appreciated. Which is not to say that my husband doesn't appreciate me. It's more, just, how much can you possibly appreciate someone when you've been together for twenty-three fucking years? And having someone really thoughtful and funny and smart see me anew was just mind-boggling. I have been a party to other infidelities, but mostly I found these men essentially convenient penises. This is the first person with whom I've felt a rapport that went past the sexual. And that scares me.

So I guess my question is this: I know this was a one-(two-) time deal and that I need to just let it be a thing that was and feel bad about it and move on, but I'm finding it impossible to do. I think about this guy all the time—like, most seconds of the day. It's distracting me from being a good partner to my husband, from being a person who can work and create, from everything. Do you have any tips for letting go? I love who I have, and I am pretty much content with the compromises I have made. Why should one lovely afternoon with a lovely guy I will probably never see again and who has no lasting interest in me fuck everything up? (Except because I'm an asshole who deserves it.)

Wish I Wasn't Such a Terrible Person

—∿∿—

Dear WIWSATP,

I get a little self-righteous when it comes to infidelity. In any committed, exclusive relationship, even a troubled one, having sex with someone else might feel casual and even unrelated to your spouse, but to your spouse it's like this act of violence has been committed against his or her psyche. I know you feel guilty, but I want to start there because I think people let themselves off the hook a lot on this front without taking full measure of the emotional impact of their actions. An event like this can really fuck with a person's sense of well-being as well as his or her perspective on the past and the future. Cheating is never a small thing, even if you and your husband have both done it before.

That said, I think it's also obvious that being with the same person since you were eighteen carries with it a particular set of challenges. I don't think I know a single couple who've been together since their early twenties who haven't struggled with some form of cheating or some talk of open marriages. And many of the couples I know who met when they were very young have trouble not reverting to that age when issues arise. They can go through years of couples therapy, they can be mature outside of the relationship, but when it comes to confronting each other, they suddenly turn into teenagers. (Hell, even close friendships can turn that way. A friend of mine from junior high school and I practically had to go through couples therapy ourselves.)

So I would never sit in judgment of anyone who's managed to keep a marriage together since he or she was a teenager. I was a lunatic as a teenager, I was an angry drunk in my twenties, I had boundary issues through my thirties, and I'm still no cup of tea on bad days. If I had married all the dudes I wanted to marry over the course of those years, I'd be three or four times divorced by now, with plenty of cheating along the way.

Big preamble to the central point, but stay with me: This event is a wake-up call for you. You're starting to feel unappreciated, lost, unimportant, invisible. This is the natural—or maybe not-so-natural—outcome of spending over two decades with a person you met at a very young age, and it's also the outcome of living in a culture where women are widely considered over-the-hill/damaged goods/rotten fruit at age thirty-five. Obviously, you feel good, and you probably look good, too. But no matter how great your life is, there's reckoning to be done as you approach forty.

The challenge for you right now is to pay attention to the wake-up call itself—*I need something else from my life!*—rather than getting distracted by the memory of hot sex and the seductive cloud of illusion that floats around the edges of extreme fame. One of the really dangerous things about famous people is that they ooze a sense of importance. If you are being seen by someone the world sees, somehow you matter. If you are being adored and ravaged by this SEEN person, suddenly you are no longer invisible. You are the sexy heroine lingering between the sheets in the suspense thriller. You are full color, larger-than-life, brilliant and special and vivid and amazing.

This, of course, is also how it feels to have great sex. This is the sensation of being ravished: You matter. You are fully awake and alive. Your ego is fed and your senses are fed at the same time. When you put yourself into that mind-set, when you try that on for size, it's not all that hard to see why people are obsessed with sex, why people cheat, why some people will do almost anything for that fix, even if it tears their lives apart.

So you have the double whammy of fame and hot sex seducing you into feeling like you had this brief taste of super-powered, all-encompassing everythingness. But just as actual famous people don't maintain this level of ecstasy over being famous for long, real relationships don't match the ecstasy of an affair. Your experience was seductive and magical, but that doesn't mean it's something that could exist outside of the confines of a hotel room or your imagination.

And who is this famous guy, really? Is he a wonderful person who just happens to be single and just happens to think you're attractive and just happens not to mind that you've been married forever? Is he a perfectly satisfied guy who fucks around a lot because, well, he can? Or is having sex with women who admire him what he does to make it through the day?

Even though it doesn't sound like you'd leave your husband for him, even if that were even an option, maybe it makes sense to imagine what that would be like. What would it be like to have sex with him over and over again and travel the world being the girlfriend of a super-famous dude? Would it be magical? Would you feel SEEN and IMPORTANT forever? Would you get to be the sexy heroine lingering between the sheets in the suspense thriller, full color, larger-than-life, brilliant and special and vivid and amazing, forever and ever? Would it be good enough to feel that way for a year? Two years? And then, maybe, you'd be replaced with an upgrade. Would it all be worth it?

Who knows? Maybe it would be incredible. For our purposes, though, I want to propose that it wouldn't be so electric for even one more night. You say you felt seen. I think you'd wake up the next day and see how good he is at making everyone, from you to some kid on the street, feel seen. I don't think you'd feel more appreciated and more full-color than you do with your husband over the long haul. I think you would feel LESS so. You say yourself that the problem isn't that your husband doesn't appreciate you. You have no major complaints about him.

So this is really about you. You're in your early forties, and you want your life to be bigger. WHO DOESN'T?! We all want our lives to be gigantic. Maybe that's a flaw of our screwy, self-centered culture. Maybe we all thought we would be superhero princesses, painting murals and flying to Monaco and firing giant weapons and riding on the backs of orcas into the sunset. Maybe we thought we'd stay young and special and fabulous forever and it would only get better and better.

It's not hard to meet someone who's successful and attractive and have the faintest sense that if that person is attracted to you, too, that means you are somehow MEANT TO LIVE AMONG THE GOLDEN PEOPLE. I get that. I interviewed celebrities when I was younger, and sometimes my mind was prone to these slightly toxic, self-involved flights of fancy. But you know what? Life is just life, for all of us. There is no golden life. We all have to face ourselves, every day. No amount of fame or money in the world can cushion you from the mundane trials of everyday existence. Those who believe otherwise are young and naive, and they fundamentally misunderstand this world. When someone says, "What does she care? She's rich!" I really question that person's onboard navigation system. Hang out with a few rich people and a few famous people, and you'll see. They are not immune.

And getting that full-colored, full-body rush over being alive and being seen and being SOMEBODY? You can have that. This guy gave you a taste of something that you already own, something that's been asleep inside you for a long time. You don't need to kick your husband to the curb to have that feeling back. Do you see that? The most important thing is to honor the part of your soul that woke up when you strayed.

When you have been "good" for years—stayed loyal to your husband for a long time, been a helpful partner, fulfilled the demands of your career, showed up for your friends—it's totally natural for something deep inside you to crave wildness and darkness and things that you haven't been able to even acknowledge for ages. Your soul might want to let in some of the seemingly BAD emotions: anger and resentment and selfishness. I'm not talking about kicking kittens, either. I'm talking about acknowledging a desire to be alone, to be seen as a separate person, to go to a party without a mate by your side, to make art, to write angry things, to learn a new language, to complain, to dye your hair a new color, to wear tall boots, to play guitar, to tell people to go away, to be a little bigger and pushier than you were before.

All of this may sound like the stuff of adolescence. But sometimes in our lives we have to dare to try on the other side of things, just to see what fits. Sometimes, when there's a crisis, it means the life we're leading is starting to chafe.

Don't go throwing out everything at once or decide that you've been brought back to life by this super-famous magic man. People latch onto narratives like that so easily. I promise: It's a mirage. Unless you're truly trapped in a terrible, irredeemable marriage (this doesn't sound like you), it's smart to be suspicious of the sensation that an affair will deliver you from stagnation. Many a truly terrible marriage has been wrought from the ashes of a pretty good, redeemable one.

You've learned something here: You've learned that you need more from your life. You made a mistake, but along the way you've been given an invitation to answer the lonely bleatings of your neglected soul. You are stepping into a new era now. Separate this famous guy from your vision, and think about what it means to feel intimate with other people, to feel connected to them, to feel appreciated by them. You need closer friendships that are more intimate and meaningful to you. You need a closer relationship with yourself. You need to feel sexier and wilder and more alive in your everyday life. You need to explore and discover new things. You need to see that this is the start of a great new chapter of your life, and it can be anything under the sun. Do you feel that? You are already full color, larger-than-life, brilliant and special and vivid and amazing. You have to feel your way, through small changes and big changes, through little risks and big ones, through speaking your mind and listening more, to a new reality and a new life. You are not an asshole. You don't want to fuck everything up. You just want to be seen. You want to treat yourself to a new way of living, one that honors you, one that's honest and real and doesn't involve sneaking around or hiding in plain sight. You aren't a terrible person, so make the choice not to act like one ever again. Treat yourself with the respect and love that you deserve.

Polly

The Good Wife

Dear Polly,

I am a thirty-eight-year-old emergency dispatcher. I have known my wife for ten years, and we have been married for the last six years. We have a wonderful three-year-old son together.

During the course of our marriage, my wife would subtly make hints about how I was not home enough, that I did not help out around the house enough, and, after our son was born, that I was not taking as active a role as she would have liked in parenting. You see, I have always been the type of person who is *not* a homebody, and my wife is the exact opposite. I would go out with my friends very often; she was always invited but would simply say no. When our son was born, she pointed this out, and I scaled back my time with my friends substantially, or so I thought. I used to go out every weekend. I scaled it back to three times a month.

This past Christmas, we were spending the holiday with family, and while out to dinner she began to ask me if I wanted more kids. I told her that I did, and we began to work out when we could start to try to get pregnant again. Three weeks after Christmas, she tells me that she wants to get separated because I am not home and I'm not helping out around the house enough. She says that she has grown unhappy in our marriage.

I realize that this unhappiness is all my fault, and I am scared that I ruined the best thing that ever happened to me.

I asked her if I made the changes that she is asking for, would she stay, and she told me that she does not know. That maybe it would work but she does not know.

I do not want this marriage to end, because I love her more now than I did when we were first married. I guess what I am asking is if the marriage is worth saving. I also don't understand why three weeks after talking to me about having another child she would tell me this.

Hope you can help.

Afraid That I Ruined the Best Thing

—m—

Dear ATIRTBT,

Your wife's hints weren't subtle, trust me. The fact that you've shrugged and said, "Well, you're a homebody and I'm not," to someone who's at home watching a toddler and grappling with a sink full of dirty dishes and a pile of dirty laundry suggests that you have an astounding ability to ignore the facts on the ground while blithely continuing along whatever path you choose. I'm guessing that you wrote off your wife's repeated "hints" (see also her deepest desires and wishes, delivered through tears, with a great deal of urgency in her voice), chalked them up as nagging, then exited to sip beers with your bros while she held it down at home.

You weren't listening. You lacked empathy. You shrugged her off. Finally, you agreed (reluctantly, I'm guessing) to cut back your weekend excursions from four a month to three a month. You saw this as a big sacrifice. You made that clear to her.

If you took an active role with your kid, if you cleaned up after yourself, if you felt terrible when your wife told you she felt buried under the weight of her domestic chores and needed a break, if you offered to watch your son at night, if you started to clean up much more often, if you encouraged your wife to take a break and go see her friends and go away for a weekend? Then she wouldn't be wondering if you're a human being with a functioning brain and heart. But you didn't do any of those things. You took her desperation and sadness and frustration and shrugged it off as just another wife bitching about her husband. (*All wives do that. Amirite, bro? Fist bump.*)

I know I'm being harsh, but if you're going to save your marriage, you need to wake the fuck up and see how completely weak and lame and passive you're being, and have probably been for years. When one person is handling the overwhelming majority of the domestic load for three years while his/her wife/husband/partner hits the town every weekend and refuses to stay home and watch the fort (or clean the fort!), guess what? The one who's left at home gets angrier and angrier until there's not much love left.

Is your marriage worth saving? If you love her more than ever and you feel like you might've ruined the best thing that ever happened to you, why are you even asking me that? Did you really think I'd say, "Nah, man, forget that whiny bitch! Who needs her?" Do you seriously not understand why she'd be asking you if you want another kid? She's wondering if you even love her enough to want another kid, since the main thing you seem to enjoy is hanging with your buddies on weekends. She's wondering how in the world she'd manage at home with two kids and no help. She's wondering what you have left together. She's wondering why, if she's doing ALL of the work anyway, she doesn't just bail while she's young so she can find another guy who actually enjoys spending time with her. Maybe she could find a guy who knows how to load a dishwasher and vacuum and get up in the middle of the night to deal with a three-year-old's bad dreams. Maybe she could have another baby with a guy who acts like he's in love with her and listens to her and takes her feelings into account instead of writing them off as "subtle hints."

What's sad is that so many men end up where you are now without knowing how they got there. They assume that once you marry a woman, she's going to stick by your side, cook your meals, raise your kids, and deal with pretty much every single thing on the home front all week, only to sit around at home on the weekends alone while you go off and have your fun. Women don't have to live that way. They have other options. Your wife shouldn't have to threaten you with divorce for you to know that.

Maybe she really was being subtle. Maybe she didn't put her foot down and say, "Come on, guy. It's the WEEKEND. Ever think about, I don't know, FINDING US A SITTER AND MAKING A DINNER RESERVATION? Ever think about STAYING HOME WHILE I GO OUT? Ever think AT ALL?" I feel bad for dudes who can't listen and can't take their ladies seriously unless they're screaming and crying. Because this is where it ends: with a wife who can't feel anything anymore. You ignore a person's emotions for years and years, and guess what? They have no emotions left for you.

I know you don't like hearing it. I'm sure there are things you do to help that I'm not considering—how you watch your kid on weekends for a little while, or play a bit of ball in the yard, or occasionally fold a load of laundry while you're watching *SportsCenter*. I'm sure you're not a bad guy. But if you want to save your marriage, listen to me: You need to drop everything and woo your wife. Tell her you're sorry. Tell her you're willing to do your share of the cleaning. Tell her you're willing to watch the kid every other weekend while *she* goes out. Tell her you'll hire a sitter every Saturday night instead of going out with your buddies so you two can go out instead. Tell her you'll go to couples therapy with her. Tell her you'll redesign your entire marriage from the ground up.

This isn't a moment to wonder what's worth saving. Your wife is great. Your life is great. The only thing that's bad about this picture is *you*. ARE YOU WORTH SAVING? Ask yourself that instead. Then figure out how to save yourself. Figure out how to be a better person, a better listener, a better friend, a better husband, a better partner. Figure out how to show up and do your share. Figure out how to shower your wife with the love and affection that she deserves.

The best thing that ever happened to you is about to go sour permanently. This isn't a time for wishy-washiness and second-guessing. This is a time to take action. This is a time for great big flowery gestures and gifts and long, heartfelt letters. Don't expect her to come around instantly, either. Be patient. Don't get mad if she doesn't immediately start kissing your ass just for being nice for a few days or weeks or months. You've been lazy and blind for a long, long time, Afraid. It's probably going to take a long, long time to win her back. But this is a crucial moment in your life. This is the part where you grow up, at long last. This is the part where you learn just how good it can feel to put someone else first.

Polly

Full Disclosure

Dear Polly,

I've got a *real* doozy. It involves my past coming back to haunt me and possibly admitting a big failure to my boyfriend (I've never told anyone, because I'm so ashamed).

Here's the story: About four years ago, I was seduced by a married man who was my superior at work in my small town. It was a textbook affair: He was well respected in my field, offered to mentor me (but at a sexual price), made four times my salary (was more "valuable" than I), told me his marriage was doomed and that he'd leave his wife. Yes, I fell for it. I resisted his advances for a full year but was afraid to report him to HR because I was desperate to learn more in a very competitive career. I even have digital evidence (text messages, chats) of the whole situation, but I never submitted them, because I was young, stupid. He took my lack of complaint as consent and was relentless in his advances, and over time I started to believe his lies.

It took a while to get physical, but as soon as it did, I woke up and realized he would never leave his wife. I felt incredibly guilty, so I quit my job, demanded no contact, didn't date for two years, and eventually forgave myself.

The problem: My current, equal-partnership, nontoxic, wonderful boyfriend (of two years) may accept a job at the same firm where my former "mentor" works. It's a great opportunity, but he could get hired elsewhere because he is talented. My boyfriend knows that my mentor works there and that my mentor sexually harassed me for months. What he doesn't know is that I eventually did cave in to my mentor's advances. However, I was too ashamed to tell my boyfriend the whole truth, and neither of us really shares specifics on our sexual history because neither of us are very interested in details of our romantic pasts.

The question: Should I tell my boyfriend everything? Our industry is small, and the "mentor" may eventually figure out our connection. If my boyfriend works with him, is it more kind for him to know the truth? Or perhaps decide that he shouldn't go work there, even though it's a great company? Or, the worst-case scenario for me, decide that he and I are no longer a good fit as a couple?

If I should tell my boyfriend, do I tell him now? Or should I wait until he makes a decision? If he decides to go elsewhere, is it okay that I keep this buried in my past?

I've privately atoned for this sin, and I hate that it's a part of my past. I've gotten older, stronger, wiser, kinder. This time, I want to do the right thing. But this situation is a painful, humbling reminder that I did the wrong thing once and that fear/embarrassment is clouding my judgment. What's the best way to handle this?

Sincerely,
Regrets Die Hard

—m—

Dear RDH,

You should definitely tell your boyfriend right now—immediately, *today*. This is not the shameful revelation that you think it is. You're just too close to it to see that. Plus, you've never told anyone, so you haven't put things in perspective effectively. You were a young, naive woman worried about your future, and you were in an imbalanced power dynamic with a charismatic creep who told you lies and relentlessly seduced you for a full year. I mean, Jesus, the effort some fuckers will go to, just to pry open one pair of lady pants! Why doesn't someone that busy and important have fulfilling hobbies so he doesn't have to waste all his time wheedling and cajoling near teenagers into serving up the goods?

Obviously, I don't encourage affairs with married men or bosses or married bosses (bleccch), but it's not exactly shocking that you might've found yourself slowly but surely succumbing to the fantasy of a life on easy street via a soon-to-be-divorced boss man. He was relentless, and he planted a seed in your head that you two were destined to be a pair. He was manipulative. He complained about his wife. He acted like maybe you two were soul mates. He acted like the attraction between you was white-hot. He treated you like the one ray of sunshine in his life. A TALE AS OLD AS TIME.

But look, you held out for a full year. And you didn't date for two years after that. Even though *you* weren't the one who made marriage vows and broke them just to feed your hungry dipshit ego, I'll bet you're the one who's feeling the most shame over it now. It's amazing how that works, isn't it? He invests an entire year trying to lure you into the sack and betray his family, but somehow *you're* worse because you're the sucker, the slut, the one who got tricked. Why do we live in a world where manipulative bullies are treated like crafty heroes and naive youngsters with big dreams are made to feel pathetic?

Stop carrying the shame of this around with you. It's not yours to carry. It belongs to the weasel who preyed on your ambition and your naïveté. And as you look back on the two years you spent ashamed of yourself and unable to go near any other guy, release that sad young woman from this shame, too. Let her be someone else, someone who's forgiven, someone who was slowly learning some hard truths about the world. She was fooled (understandably!), but she won't get fooled again.

Take that attitude into your conversation with your boyfriend. Be honest with him, but keep in mind that even though you feel shame, you really shouldn't.

No matter how you do it, though, you *must* tell your boyfriend about this, and soon. It's very important for him to understand who this guy is before he starts working for/with him. You do NOT want him finding out after he accepts the job—or, god forbid, a year into it—that you slept with his co-worker. He may never forgive you for not telling him the truth earlier. He may be so uncomfortable and so freaked out and so furious at you that he breaks up with you, just for failing to tell him the truth for so long.

And really, it's easy enough to say to him now, "Look, I didn't think it would come to this and I didn't think there was ever any reason for you to know the full story, because I thought it would only bother you and make you feel jealous. But I need to tell you now. You should know before you make your choice."

Be clear with him about how ashamed you've felt over this, and be clear that you don't want to feel ashamed about it anymore. But be vulnerable about what you've gone through, too, so he understands what a huge, difficult situation this was for you. Let him know that you really need him to understand and support you because it's a big deal in your personal and professional life and you've been keeping it hidden from everyone for so long that it's really not healthy.

Give him some room to be freaked out. Be patient. Don't get mad at him for feeling whatever he feels about it. Then give him an opening to play the supportive boyfriend, too. I think he will. If he's a good guy, he will. Let him know that you've been losing sleep over this.

But definitely don't just cross your fingers and hope that

he picks a different job. No way. *Just tell him.* Trust me, I've known plenty of people who didn't tell their partners important things—like introducing former lovers as "old friends" in passing without thinking about it—and then the truth comes out and one really minor, stupid lie turns into what feels like a major violation of trust and a big wound that needs to be mended. When you conceal the truth, you make your past affair feel, to your boyfriend, like it still holds sexual intrigue for you. You give the impression, with a small lie, that you still DESERVE to feel shame over this.

But you don't. So don't fall into that trap. Tell him everything, and while you're at it, talk with him about the importance of honesty in a relationship. Without honesty, there really isn't a relationship at all. Don't live that way. Don't try to seem better than you are. Show him who you are, mistakes and all. That's how you'll build a solid foundation of trust between you two, so you can move forward and make a whole lifetime of mistakes *together*. (Ha!)

Tell him the truth. Then put down this load and don't pick it up again. You've carried it around for long enough.

Polly

Mourning Glory

Hi, Polly,

Last year my father, who was fifty-six, died suddenly of a heart aneurysm. He took me out for my twenty-fourth birthday dinner, and then two days later he was dead.

I feel like the past months have been a mess of every emotion possible. I'm a great big ball of pain, and it seems as though grief is the one thing no one will talk about with me. My dad was the parent who showed up for me, who supported me as a writer. We shared so many similarities: a tendency to overthink and undersleep, a need for long intellectual conversations, a deep and sometimes painful sensitivity, and a love of words.

My mother has said she can't understand why I'm so sad and depressed over my dad's death. It's a message I've gotten before, as though I'm overreacting in my grief. That I need to toughen up and get over it. I'm in therapy, but I worry about how I will ever deal with this. Can you give me any advice?

Signed,
The Daughter Left Behind

—〜—

Hi, TDLB,

Your mother can't tolerate seeing you unhappy. That's all. She's unsettled by it and worries that you'll never snap out of it.

As a mother, I can relate to that very well, and I'm sympathetic to her. She only wants you to be happy.

But—BUT!—there's a certain kind of childhood to be had in the company of someone who only wants you to be happy. Think about what that means, the flatness, the scentless sterility of that: I. Only. Want. You. To. Be. Happy.

Here's what I DON'T want you to be:

Devastated
Confused
Remorseful
Harried
Unnerved
Haunted
Inspired
Embarrassed
Tempted
Nervous
Seduced
Melancholy
Nostalgic
Grateful

Your mother doesn't want you to struggle or overthink things. She doesn't want you to be sensitive or complicated. She doesn't want you to honor exactly who you are. She wants you to GET OVER IT so she can feel at peace again. She's probably a little bit controlling. Just a guess. She's probably a little bit anxious.

And again, I understand that, and I have empathy for it, as a sometimes-anxious woman with kids. But you have to find a way to set all of her expectations and desires for you aside. You can love her and still do that. You have to find a way to get a little space for yourself, to get a little distance, so you can look back over that distance and say, "This person, my mother, is conflicted and sad in ways that she won't admit. She wants us to lie together. She will react negatively to *anything* that I do that doesn't feel absolutely safe and controlled and happy and that's not a direct reflection of what she wants for me."

Your mother doesn't want you to be an artist, a writer, an intellect. But that's what you are, right? That's what you want and what you believe in. You want the truth; you want to feel what you feel. You want to feel completely, painfully alive, and you know, instinctively, that this includes diving straight into your grief and not coming up to the surface until you feel like you're ready.

My father also died when he was fifty-six years old, completely out of the blue, from his first heart attack. He was in great shape and extremely youthful. He ran or swam every day. He was a professor of economics, prone to bizarre digressions about human nature and spirituality and also prone to aggressive, off-color jokes. He was ruled by his emotions. I don't want to imply that he and I had the same sort of relationship that you had with your father; my dad could be very difficult, and I was treated more like a sidekick than an equal. But he loved me and he showed it, and when he died, I felt like the center of my life would never return. He and I were both very needy, very raw, and the rest of my family was much more controlled, more skeptical, more reserved, far less prone to starting a fight or leaping into the fray or showing their asses. When he died, I mourned for about four months straight, and then something shifted. I turned something off. I didn't want to play my role as joker. I was the last remaining emotional wild card in my family, and I felt ashamed of that suddenly, and for the first time I withdrew. I was twenty-five years old, and after several years of drifting and drinking too much I got a boyfriend, got a great job, got in shape, and shut all the emotional neediness and messiness out for a while.

Maybe I made a decision to BE HAPPY. I wrote cartoons, and that was part of it, too; I stopped drawing attention to myself as much and drew attention to my work instead. I pushed that clown onto the page and became much more flat and controlled in real life. I dated a childlike artist, somebody who needed my help. I was strong. But I wasn't happy, not exactly.

Then I went into therapy, and I realized that two years later I hadn't grieved my father's death nearly enough. Two years of grieving, even if you're not trying to turn it off most of the time, is nothing when it comes to a parent or a spouse or anyone you've lived with for a big part of your life. When it's someone like your dad, who formed your identity? Of course you feel lost without him. You want him back. That's a gigantic loss. And it feels like you're losing part of your childhood, too, when someone important from your childhood disappears. It doesn't help that your mother doesn't understand or doesn't accept what a huge sea change you're still grappling with.

So, you need to get some distance from your mother. Forgive her, talk about her in therapy, try to lean on her, but accept that she may never get it, or she'll be too invested in your "getting over" this to get it. (Was she married to your dad when he died? It doesn't sound like it, but if she was, WHOA.) She isn't the right person to tell about the full force of your emotions. You know, mothers often can't fill this role, sadly. Many of us are just too invested in our kids' survival, and anything we perceive as threatening to that gets the heave-ho, even at the cost of their truest, fullest happiness.

No one else will talk about grief with you? See, this is the bullshit thing about suffering a big loss when you're so young. I went through this, too. Very few of my friends—and I had lots of friends—were capable of even discussing my dad's death with me. It made them uncomfortable. That's how young we were. They were sure they'd say the wrong thing. We were all so self-conscious and inflexible and confused by the immense gulf between different people's experiences. Some people stay that way, too. They try to downplay death or act like the death of a second cousin and the death of a parent should be tackled with the same blasé toughness. It happens; you get over it. And if you talk about someone else's death, about how it affected or affects you? That's self-involved and pathetic.

Not only is this attitude bizarre, insensitive, and pathologically self-protective, but it shuts out the possibility that maybe, just maybe, you don't know that much about death yet because you've never had a close friend or family member die. When you lose someone very close to you, someone who makes up this essential part of your history and your future, your worldview shifts dramatically. You have a palpable feeling that everything and anything good can disappear at any time. I missed my dad a lot. I also felt like everyone I knew was going to start dying. I also hated that my dad wasn't able to go on living. I wanted him to be alive; I wanted him to feel rain on his face, to eat a great meal, to read something funny, for HIS sake.

After my dad's death, I felt more anguished *and* I felt more alive than I'd ever felt in my life. I felt more grateful than ever. I only wanted honest people in my life, people who could talk about heaviness and melancholy and really savor it instead of feeling uncomfortable. I don't think I stuck to that. I think I couldn't handle staying in that space for very long, because it made me feel too raw. So I retreated.

Don't retreat. You need to find people who will talk about this. Figure out who they are. You're in therapy now. If your therapist isn't helping you deal with this very well, then get a new therapist. Or find a grief counselor, too. Or find a therapy group for people mourning a big loss. Look hard at your friends, and figure out which ones you can lean on a little more. Someone out there can handle it, I'm sure of that. You just have to figure out who it is.

And you need to write things down. Every day. It'll help you to understand what shape your pain takes so it doesn't take you by surprise, so you can talk yourself out of feeling paralyzed by it.

You also need to exercise every day. Mourning and exercise go very well together. You're already in a lot of pain—what's a little more? Fatigue can feel pretty redemptive when you're sad.

Because mourning is about being alive. That's something you have to remind yourself of, and maybe you should even take a shot at trying to explain this to your mother. Leaning into your sadness is not refusing to be happy. Leaning into your sadness, every day, inviting it into your life, getting up and putting on some running shoes and running and walking and running for an hour or two, and crying while you run or walk—that's reaffirming that you want to keep living. That's celebrating how much your father meant to you and how he will never disappear from your life, ever. That's knowing that you will survive this and you'll carry it with you and it'll be a big piece of who you are.

Because you don't ONLY want to be happy. You are not a two-dimensional cartoon cutout who keeps all pain at bay, at the expense of your very soul. You are not someone who will tell other people to take their own complex, difficult, colorful experiences, experiences that you don't know anything about, and push them down, store them away, bury them, because it makes you uncomfortable. You are going to feel this crushing loss for as long as you need to feel it, you're going to feel the full force of it, so that you can also feel

Devastated
Confused
Remorseful
Harried

Unnerved
Haunted
Inspired
Embarrassed
Tempted
Nervous
Seduced
Melancholy
Nostalgic
Grateful

You *are* going to feel grateful. This is the paradox of mourning. Incredible sadness carries with it an ability to touch the purest strain of joy, to experience an almost ecstatic release, to see an almost blinding, undiluted beauty in everything. Your dad will always be a part of your life. I hated it when people said that kind of thing before my dad died; I thought it was a sad lie told by needy liars. But it's true.

Two days after my dad died, I called his insurance agent to cancel his car insurance. The guy had a thick southern accent. He didn't get all stiff and weird on the phone, like most people did. He said, "My god. He was just in here the other day. He looked so healthy and young." It was a very honest response. Then he said, "My dad died when I was twenty-five years old. That was twenty-five years ago. I still remember him perfectly, like I just saw him yesterday. I still have dreams about him." At the time, I thought that sounded incredibly heartbreaking and depressing.

But here it is, almost twenty years later, and I get it. I remember my dad perfectly—his big laugh, his voice singing "Danny Boy" with showy bravado, his teasing tones, his little Muhammad Ali dance. If I turn my back on how important he is, I block my path to joy. I block my ability to bring joy to other people. He is a vital part of my life. And even the sadness

I feel about losing him is vital. It makes every color brighter; it makes every single moment of happiness—or longing, or satisfaction, or grace, or melancholy—more real, more palpable, more complete.

Don't wonder how you will deal with this. You ARE dealing with it. Don't wonder how you will get over it. You will NEVER get over it. I know that seems heartbreaking and depressing and wrong. Trust me that it's also gratifying and miraculous and astonishing and endlessly inspiring and important and helpful. Letting this pain in and growing from it will give you strength and resilience that you can pass on to other people in ways you can't possibly understand now. It's NOT all about you, not remotely. You are not stuck. You are not wallowing. This is a beautiful, terrible time in your life that you'll always remember. Don't turn away from it. Don't shut it down. Don't get over it.

Polly

The Bean Eaters

Hi, Polly,

Something I say a lot in therapy is "I don't know how to think about this" (my therapist, frustratingly, doesn't seem to like to tell me how to think about things—just nods and nods—but your column is good for that), and here is something I don't know how to think about:

I have a very close friend whose whole family is from a once-great and bustling American city which now has a really shitty economy and no good job prospects for the old-timers. The city declared bankruptcy in the last year. His parents, entrepreneurs, both lost their jobs and businesses (through a combination of the financial crisis, the city collapsing, sheer bad luck, and risky decision-making) and eventually lost their house as they fell behind on mortgage payments. They used to be doing well, were comfortable, and now they have bad health and live off family, quite depressed, with a mountain of debt. They do these small jobs, but nothing in this city really pays well enough to get them back on track and in their own place. I also think they are defeated and exhausted, and the people around them sense this defeat and want very little to do with it, like it might be catching.

They are in their late fifties, have an ill parent who keeps them in the city (although I don't know where they would go even so), and my friend says it's so hard to watch this slow-motion disaster. My friend is doing okay, but not okay enough to be of much financial help, but he tries. He says it's just difficult to know that you can get older and—contrary to much popular wisdom—things can get much harder. That life is a struggle, getting older is difficult and heartbreaking, your body gives out, and complete uncertainty and failure is what we have to look forward to. What's the point?? It's so hard to have the energy and motivation to remake your life past a certain point. And is it even possible?

I agree that sometimes I don't know the point when I see situations like this. It looks hopeless. I struggle with depression, and it depresses me more. And also I don't know the right things to say in response to all this loss, to make it less awful, make sense of it, frame it in a way that isn't totally devastating. My friend's parents have each other (they're both very sweet people) and two great kids. But it doesn't feel like enough right now. Is there a right thing to say?? What is the point??

How Do I Make Sense of This

—✺—

Dear HDIMSOT,

On the first day of class in tenth grade, my English teacher asked me to read a poem out loud in class. I was about to start when she spotted my last name in her book and said, "Hmmm. I bet you think you're clever, because of your sister." (My older sister was the valedictorian.) "Well," she continued, "what you *don't* know is that your brother is the smartest one in your family." (My older brother looked like Shaggy from *Scooby-Doo!*, got middling grades, and put all of his energy into playing D&D on the weekends.) "Anyway, go ahead and read."

Right. So now let's see if the dumbest little fuck in the family can manage to say a few words out loud without screwing up. The poem was "The Bean Eaters," by Gwendolyn Brooks.

In it, Brooks tells the story of an old, poor couple who eat their dinner of beans off chipped plates.

When I was finished reading, my teacher asked what I thought the poem was about. I looked down at the page again, panicking. This old couple had lived past their expiration date, Brooks seems to say. Even so, they kept getting dressed and straightening up and tinkering about their little rented room. That sounded pretty empty. Their lives were basically over, as far as I could tell, but they were still going through the motions. All they had left were their memories. They remember "with twinklings and twinges," Brooks writes, as they eat their beans in a room packed with "beads and receipts and dolls and cloths" and also "tobacco crumbs, vases and fringes."

Those words reminded me of my grandmother, who was having trouble with her memory and was a serious pack rat. We had just moved her out of her house in Chicago that summer so she could come to live with us. She had closets full of yogurt lids and empty glass jars and old newspapers, all saved for some imaginary art project that would never happen. Clearing out that house was one of the most depressing things I'd ever done: All of her plans were up in smoke, her life was basically over, and she didn't even know what year it was.

So, I cleared my throat. "Well . . . the poem is about having no money and having no control over your life," I said. "These poor people are surrounded by their own filth—chipped plates, tobacco crumbs—and they're basically just waiting to die."

"NOOOOOOO!" my teacher screeched, standing up and slamming her gnarled fist down on her desk. "NO, NO, NO, NO, NO!" she bellowed, pounding her fist onto the desk over and over with each "NO." Then she got up and stood right in front of me and pointed a scary finger in my face and fixed me with two ferocious eyes.

"That is WRONG. You got it ALL WRONG. They are poor, but they are *happy*! You think they have to be miserable just because they're POOR?! THEY HAVE THEIR MEMORIES! TWINKLINGS AND TWINGES! What do you think those are? *TWINKLINGS! AND! TWINGES!* YOU DON'T EVEN *KNOW*, DO YOU?!" She returned to her desk and sat down. "Oh, you kids are so spoiled. You're so, so, so spoiled! It makes me sick, it really does. You don't have any sense of anything."

So, that went really well.

But let's get to the point, which isn't actually that this fine nation of ours is filled with crumbling, once-great American cities packed with crumbling, once-great public schools that employ once-great teachers (who eventually become world-weary sadists with boundary issues, amirite?). The real point is that when you're young and you're a little depressed and you're not sure what will make your life feel rich and fulfilling and worthwhile, it's pretty impossible to understand how it feels to have lived a full life already.

That's not me calling all of the youngest ones the dumbest ones, either. That's me saying that YOU are the one we need to worry about in this picture, not your friend's parents. Because where you are right now is extremely fucking hard. It's tough to start down the path to adult life with even the slightest whiff of depression on board. And, honestly, it's hard for even the happiest, cheeriest person alive to navigate their twenties *without* becoming depressed.

When you're a little depressed, you see the world through a smoggy, gray haze. You look at older people who've lost everything and you think, "Is THAT where we all end up?" There are so many unknowns in your life right now. So, when you look at older people who are also facing unknowns, it just buries you. Is there no relief from feeling lost? Even if you *do* figure things out and get a house and a job and a life, it could all be taken away from you in a heartbeat! So, what's the fucking point?

Listen to me: You don't know how bad it is for them, but

you also don't know how good it is for them. I know they're only in their late fifties—which really isn't old, by the way. I guarantee they've navigated a few hardships already. They've experienced disappointments. Yes, I'm sure they're depressed and overwhelmed right now. But they're nice people, and they have each other. They have "an ill parent who keeps them in the city." To you, that sounds like one more shitty thing in their lives, and I understand that. But sometimes having a big responsibility can actually *help* you make it through the hard times.

Let's go back to those twinklings and twinges from the poem. When I was young, I breezed right past that line, but there's joy in those words that I couldn't detect. And even once my teacher shouted at me, I still thought, "Oh, yeah? What's so good about having your memories? What's so good about being surrounded by beads and dolls, vases and fringes? That sounds horribly claustrophobic and depressing!"

Part of the satisfaction of getting older, though, comes from feeling connected—deeply connected—to other people and to yourself. Your friends' parents are still showing up for this ill parent, and they're showing up for each other. Maybe they're arguing every night in some relative's guest room or even on the fold-out couch in some living room. I don't know. But they're together, living through this as a couple, even as some of their closest friends back away from them.

You're sensitive, which is a nice quality. You're alarmed by how their friends could abandon them. Pay attention to that part, because it's one of the most devastating things you learn as you get older: Some of the most loyal-seeming friends in the world will end up bailing on you when things get tough. Sometimes it means they didn't love you in the first place and you just didn't know it before. But other times it's just pathological: I Hate Feeling Uncomfortable, So I Avoid Heaviness At All Costs.

Now *you'll* never be like that. Now that you've seen that up close, you know you'll never be a person who doesn't show up for a close friend. Maybe this couple was reckless with their money, and maybe they weren't. It doesn't matter. Never use an "I told you so" attitude to let yourself off the hook from showing up for someone you love. And don't use the "I don't know what to say" excuse, either, or the "I'm afraid I'll say something wrong" excuse. You probably *will* say something wrong. That's okay. JUST SHOW UP. Show up and say, "God, this sucks. I'm so sorry." Just keep saying that, and keep showing up.

Your friend *is* showing up. He's concerned, and he's trying to help. Don't underestimate how big that is, having a son who wants to help you. A parent in that situation might think, "*We* should be helping *him*! We've squandered his inheritance!" Fuck inheritances. It's beautiful that their son wants to help, and his parents can feel that, even though they're in pain. Your friend just needs to keep showing that he loves them and that he's grateful for all that they've already done for him. He needs to give them the gift of his words. Two sweet people will treasure that more than he can possibly imagine.

And yet, it's also true what your friend says: You get older, and, contrary to popular wisdom, things do get much harder. Popular wisdom is usually complete horseshit in fact. Mostly it's designed to keep us from freaking out about how bleak everything actually is. We're spoon-fed this diet of enforced cheer in the form of pop songs and chirpy sitcoms and TV commercials to keep us on a straight and narrow path of docile consumption and compliance, while the world goes straight to hell. And the sad fact is that we ALL get older and older, and we don't have the money we imagined we'd have, and we're never quite as fabulous as we imagined we'd be. And then on top of it all, the debts start piling up, and our hair starts turning gray, and our balance of days on earth gets shorter. And one day we look in the mirror, and we say to ourselves, "Fuck, *am I ugly*! And I feel *terrible*. And it's only going to get worse from here!"

Yep. Growing old is a motherfucker. Three years ago, a friend of mine died, and I felt sick about it, and I was losing sleep over money issues, and my writing felt stuck. And when I looked in the mirror (rarely!), I saw an angry old lady with dark circles under her eyes, but when I tried to put on makeup to fix the problem, I just looked like an angry old hooker instead. (I mean sex worker. See how old?)

Life is a struggle. But that Summer of Feeling Old, I flew home to my mom's house, and instead of feeling annoyed by my mom, I stayed quiet. I noticed how organized she was and saw how she took walks or went to her exercise class every single day. I noticed the new watercolor of her dog that she'd painted and framed. And then she made this great salad with stilton and pine nuts and some cold beet soup for dinner one night, and she poured us glasses of wine, and she told us about the birds she'd been seeing at the bird feeder outside her big window, and then she played the kids some birdcalls from the special audio bird book she has. "Let's find the eastern towhee," she said. "That's the one that sings, 'Drink your TEE-HEE-HEE-HEE-EA!'"

I'd always assumed my mom was a little unhappy and maybe a little lonely. She's old, she lives alone, why wouldn't she be, right? That night I realized I was wrong, that my mom was happy. She'd struggled mightily to save enough for retirement on a secretary's salary, and she pulled through some hard stuff. And now she was savoring her life, full stop.

Life is a struggle, but you know what? Most of us just keep rolling along one way or another, difficult or not. Sometimes, just like Gwendolyn Brooks wrote, you just have to keep getting dressed and straightening up, without questioning it.

I'll bet your friend's parents haven't given up yet. Uncertainty and failure might look like the end of the road to you. But uncertainty is a part of life. Facing uncertainty and failure doesn't always make people weaker and weaker until they give up. Sometimes it wakes them up, and it's like they can see the beauty around them for the first time. Sometimes losing everything makes you realize how little you actually need. Sometimes losing everything sends you out into the world to breathe in the air, to pick some flowery weeds, to take in a new day.

Because this life is full of promise, always. It's full of beads and dolls and chipped plates; it's full of twinklings and twinges. It *is* possible to admit that life is a struggle and also embrace the fact that small things—like sons who call you and beloved dogs in framed pictures and birds that tell you to drink your fucking tea—matter. They matter a lot.

Stop trying to make sense of things. You can't think your way through this. Open your heart and drink in this glorious day. You are young, and you will find little things that will make you grateful to be alive. Believe in what you love now, with all of your heart, and you will love more and more until everything around you is love. Love yourself now, exactly as sad and scared and flawed as you are, and you will grow up and live a rich life and show up for other people, and you'll know exactly how big that is.

Let's celebrate this moment together. There are twinklings and twinges, right here, in this moment. It is enough. Let's find the eastern towhee.

Polly

Acknowledgments

I am grateful to Yaniv Soha for recognizing the potential of this book and guiding it with wisdom, heart, and careful attention that went far beyond the call of duty. Thanks also to Bill Thomas, the ever-helpful and wise Margo Shickmanter, and the whole team at Doubleday.

I am deeply indebted to Stella Bugbee and Molly Fischer of *New York* magazine's *The Cut* for embracing Ask Polly without reservation, and for their calm guidance and grace under pressure. Thanks also to Adam Moss, David Wallace-Wells, Lauren Kern, and Lauren Starke, for their enthusiasm and support. Working for a publication that's so supportive of its writers has been a dream come true.

Massive thanks to Penelope Metcalfe for the gorgeous illustrations used in this book. Choire Sicha and Alex Balk, cofounders of *The Awl*, agreed to publish my advice column sight unseen, and wonderful *Awl* editors Carrie Frye and Matt Buchanan improved it every week. A huge thank-you also goes to the readers of *The Awl*, whose early encouragement and loyalty were beyond compare.

Meghan Daum and Lisa Glatt offered their help and feedback many times during the writing of this book, and I'm so grateful to have them as friends. Sincere thanks to Apryl Lundsten, Andrea Russell, Perri Kersh, Carina Chocano, and Ken Basart for their support and love.

I am enormously thankful to have such an amazing and generous literary agent in Sarah Burnes. She always knows just how to proceed and always makes time for my petty troubles. Thank you also to Logan Garrison for her tireless help.

A huge debt of gratitude is owed to my mother, Susan Havrilesky, for inspiring so much of what is written here with her vulnerability, her honesty, and her resilience in the face of many obstacles. Thank you also to Eric Havrilesky, Laura Havrilesky, Melissa Hernandez, Jeff Welch, Hilda Newberry, and Jean Gould for tolerating me over many decades.

My husband, Bill, is my favorite editor and also the best person I know, hands down. I am incredibly lucky to have him in my life.

Thank you to Ivy, Claire, and Zeke for putting up with me. I hope you might get some worthwhile guidance from this book as you grow older and have less interest in listening to me hold forth in person. It's not easy to do the things you dream of doing. Sometimes it's not that easy just to get up in the morning. That's how it is for everyone. Keep believing in yourself and keep accepting yourself, flaws and all. Never give up on the things and the people you love the most.

About the Author

Heather Havrilesky writes *New York* magazine's Ask Polly advice column and *Bookforum*'s Best-Seller List column. She is the author of the memoir *Disaster Preparedness* (Riverhead, 2011). She was Salon.com's TV critic for seven years and co-created the cartoon *Filler* for Suck .com, the Web's first daily site. Her writing has appeared in *The New Yorker*, the *New York Times Magazine*, *The Baffler*, *O* magazine, NPR's *All Things Considered*, and several anthologies. She lives in Los Angeles with her husband, Bill; her daughters, Claire and Ivy; and her dogs, Potus and Bean.